Food From
The Place Below

by *Bill Sewell*

with Ian Burleigh and Frances Tomlinson

Thorsons
An Imprint of HarperCollins *Publishers*

Thorsons
An Imprint of HarperCollins*Publishers*
77–85 Fulham Palace Road,
Hammersmith, London W6 8JB

Published by Thorsons 1996
1 3 5 7 9 10 8 6 4 2

A catalogue record for this book
is available from the British Library

ISBN 0 7225 3230 X

Illustrations by Leila Brieze

Printed in Great Britain by
Woolnough Bookbinding Limited
Irthlingborough, Northamptonshire

Contents

Acknowledgements

Neither the book nor the restaurant would have happened without the invaluable help of a number of people. I would especially like to thank the following:

- Tessa Strickland, my agent, who had the energy to ensure that the book developed from being a good idea to a reality
- Wanda Whiteley, at Thorsons, for receiving the proposal with enthusiasm, and Michelle Clark for her keen attention to the detail of the text
- Mary Gwynn, and everyone at BBC *Vegetarian Good Food* (where a few of these recipes first appeared), for giving me my first opportunity to write about food, and for always being encouraging about what I wrote
- Victor Stock and the congregation at St Mary-le-Bow, who have been enthusiastic about the restaurant from the start, and have proved the best imaginable landlords
- all the people who helped me during the seemingly interminable process (18 months) of setting up The Place Below, including Nick Smallwood of Launceston Place, who commented on the practicalities and showed me how a proper restaurant is run, Sarah Brown, who advised on the layout and wisely told me never to open a restaurant; and Pam Knutsen, who guided me through the opening period and provided invaluable advice and reassurance
- Ian Burleigh and Frances Tomlinson, from whom many of the ideas in this book have come, and who have kept The Place Below thriving whenever I have swanned off in pursuit of a new project
- all past and current staff of The Place Below, who have been the foundation of the restaurant's success and who constantly contribute recipes
- Charlie and Barbara Pugh, our landlords in Cornwall, who welcomed Sarah and me warmly and tested and tasted many of the recipes in this book with enthusiasm

- the many other testers and tasters, of whom special mention must go to the Girling clan (in particular Gemma, Vickie and George Green), Sarah Travis and Rob Bristow.

Lastly, I would like to thank the most important member of the Girling family, my wife, Sarah. She has given me the enthusiasm and energy to write this book. She tells me that my food is wonderful and my restaurant great, and I believe her. She makes me want to cook, to write and to enjoy the pleasures of life. Thank you, Sarah.

Introduction

I love food. My restaurant, The Place Below, is for people who love food, and so is this book. You don't have to be a vegetarian to want to eat the food in this book – most of my customers aren't vegetarian – but if you are a vegetarian, you will find nothing to offend you. It is an affirmation of the pleasures of the garden and dairy.

You will find trendy ingredients in this book (roast peppers, pesto sauce, Puy lentils), but only if they are also delicious and used in context. You will also find more traditional ingredients, but they are used in dishes that are fully flavoured and light. At The Place Below, we aim for a marriage of strong, modern flavours, using the huge variety of fresh vegetables we can now easily buy and only the best of the ingredients discovered by the wholefood pioneers – wild rice, good-quality soy sauce, fresh basil, extra virgin olive oil, good cheeses.

In *Food From The Place Below*, we hope to share some of the pleasures and secrets of this marriage with you.

From Restaurant Table to Kitchen Table

The food in this book has largely come from our lunchtime menu. Its style is dictated by the fact that, in the space of an hour and a half, we have to feed 150 customers or more from a very small kitchen. There is, therefore, very little time for elaborate last-minute finishing processes or dainty garnishes. I hope that this makes it particularly suitable for cooking at home in situations where you don't want to have a lot of last-minute faffing around, but would rather do any time-consuming preparation (if you have to do any at all) earlier in the day or even the night before.

We have spent the last six years developing the recipes in this book. Nearly all the food has been tested by hundreds, or probably more like thousands, of customers. To get it all written down, my wife Sarah and I went to Cornwall for three months (a great hardship!) to test everything in domestic quantities and using domestic equipment, and to make sure that all the ingredients were easily available outside London.

We found that with just the two of us there, something simple and quick was often what we wanted, whether for a TV dinner or because we were due in the pub in ten minutes to watch the rugby. I found this more difficult than some of you might, as (a long-running tease, this one), once I'm in the kitchen, I have a tendency to cook enough for at least 20 people. This tendency was heroically overcome, however, and is the origin of the chapter entitled Bill's Snacks. It is the one chapter that is not based on food served in the restaurant.

The restaurant food is, of course, usually cooked in much greater quantities than you might want to at home, but our style is still very much that of home cooking. We buy nothing in – bread, cakes, pastry, sauces and relishes are all made on the premises. Everything we make is fresh. At the start of the day, the restaurant is piled high with vegetables – boxes of French leaves, Spanish melons, Italian tomatoes, English apples, mushrooms and quinces. Then come the deliveries of Belgian chocolate, fresh English goats' cheese, dried ceps, Greek olive oil ... By lunchtime, all have metamorphosed into casseroles, gratins, tarts, soups, salads and luscious puds. By half past two, everything has gone and we sit down to recover, ready to start the whole process again the next day (actually, we may then go into preparation for a birthday party or celebration dinner, which might be a rather grander three- or four-course affair, or an elaborate finger buffet, but that's another story, and another cookbook).

All the recipes in this book have been designed for the ordinary home cook, so you won't need to rely on any obscure techniques or pieces of equipment. I am personally hooked on the use of an ordinary domestic food processor, but there are very few situations where it is indispensable, and I have tried to point out the few occasions where I think it is. Most of all, the recipes are designed with pleasure in mind, so I hope you enjoy them!

The Story of the Restaurant and Its People So Far

I opened The Place Below in 1989. The quest had begun seven years earlier when I told Cambridge University's careers service that I wanted to open a vegetarian restaurant. (Why couldn't I just buckle down and become an accountant?)

The restaurant is located in one of the most beautiful spaces in London – the mediaeval crypt of Wren's marvellous church, St Mary-le-Bow. The church has a vibrant weekday community and among our first and most regular customers were the rector, Victor Stock, and the members of the congregation.

One of the other customers on our first day was Ian Burleigh. He had had his own critically acclaimed vegetarian restaurant, Bart's, in Ashtead, Surrey, had been a tutor at the Vegetarian Society's cookery school and was co-author of a Sainsbury's vegetarian cookbook. Not long after that first meal, I persuaded him to come and cook at The Place Below. He has been here ever since, bringing a wealth of knowledge about food and cooking, some marvellous recipes and a warmth of personality that rubs off on all around him – both customers and staff.

As the restaurant has become busier and the rave reviews have flowed in, we have worked hard to make sure that we are always improving our food – adding new dishes, working with new ingredients and, equally importantly, developing and improving our *existing* recipes. Vital to this process has been Frances Tomlinson. Her experience of cooking for large numbers and her training at Leith's, joined with her natural sense of what tastes good, has meant a constant injection of new ideas.

We have also branched out into more elaborate cooking in the evenings – at private dinners, wedding receptions and so on – but those recipes will have to wait for the next book.

For the future, who knows? I hope that The Place Below is still near the beginning of its story. A Place Below bakery? A West End restaurant or one in the country? Watch this space, but, more importantly, enjoy this food.

Notes on Ingredients
and Using the Recipes

You cannot make horrible ingredients taste nice. Humble ingredients are, however, often the most delicious. Choose the firm and juicy carrot over the sad and withered asparagus every time.

Here are a few more specific comments.

Aubergines

Too many people think they don't like aubergines, whereas, I suspect, that all that they really mean is that they don't like *badly cooked* aubergines.

The two important things are to cook them with plenty of oil (ideally olive oil) and plenty of salt, and to cook them for long enough. In my view, pre-salting them is completely unnecessary, but cooking them for long enough and with enough oil and salt is absolutely essential. I don't like fried aubergines as they then become too oily, but grilled or, best of all, roasted, they are delicious.

Cheese

All the recipes using cheese will taste better using good cheese than using tasteless cheese. Finding a good local cheese supplier can make a real difference to your quality of eating. I live in Richmond where there is Vivian's cheese shop and deli, which is one of the best in the country. In particular, good Cheddar and Parmesan are important ingredients in quite a few of the recipes in this book. Never use the sawdust in little cardboard containers masquerading as grated Parmesan. Buy a block of the real McCoy and grate it yourself.

Strict vegetarians will only eat cheese made with vegetarian rennet. A lot of cheesemakers do not specify the type of rennet used (although, apparently, many use vegetarian rennet without stating as much), so to be absolutely safe you need to stick to cheeses that state that only non-animal rennet is used. It is not hard to find vegetarian Cheddar, Stilton and Mozzarella. It is trickier (although no longer impossible) to find vegetarian Parmesan; Avanti, made in Britain, is one which I have found to be regularly available. Vegetarian Gruyère or Roquefort we have not yet found, however.

Garlic

There are at least four quite distinct flavours to get from garlic, depending on how it is prepared, so don't give up if you have been overpowered in the past by excessive quantities of raw garlic:

- **raw garlic** the most pungent and mouth-burning way to eat garlic, as in a classic garlic mayonnaise or hummus
- **fried garlic** garlic can either be fried over a low heat to give the flavour you might associate with a garlicky tomato sauce, or fiercely so that it browns to give a more toasty flavour
- **baked or roasted garlic** this method of cooking produces a milder, nutty flavour (the baked or roasted cloves can either be eaten whole or peeled and puréed with other ingredients to make delicious dressings and sauces)
- **boiled garlic** to make garlic soup, you boil a large number of heads of garlic, then the stock and cooked garlic is strained and the resultant stock is sweet, aromatic and delicious.

When buying garlic, choose the larger and pinker bulbs and they should feel quite hard when pressed in the hand.

Herbs

In most instances, fresh herbs taste much nicer than dried herbs. In some cases (such as basil, dill, mint or parsley), the dried version is useless as a substitute. In other cases (tarragon, oregano), the dried version can be an adequate substitute, so long as it can be cooked for some time – dried herbs are never so good in uncooked food.

Mushrooms

I adore all kinds of mushrooms and they feature in many recipes in this book. There has been a welcome growth in the number of varieties of mushrooms available in supermarkets in the last few years. As well as button mushrooms and flat or field mushrooms, cultivated oyster and shiitake mushrooms are now fairly easy to get hold of. An exciting initiative is that Tesco is selling fresh wild mushrooms, and, so far, I have bought from them Chanterelles, Pied de Mouton, and Mousserons. We have not quite arrived at the French position, where they sell fresh ceps in the local grocery shop for less than the price of field mushrooms in a British supermarket, but we are getting there.

In most cases, I recommend field mushrooms for cooking – I love the flavour of the mushrooms themselves and their juice – and button mushrooms for salads, where their firm, clean texture and creamy, pale flesh is more appropriate. In a couple of cases I have suggested wild mushrooms as an alternative to field mushrooms, but do bear in mind that, even if you can get hold of them, they are likely to be at least four times the price.

The other mushroomy ingredient worth mentioning is the dried cep. In my limited experience, fresh ceps taste good but unremarkable, whereas the flavour, and especially the intense aroma, of dried ceps is something you have to smell to believe. I mention some recipe ideas on page 000, but the main point is that most of the flavour is in the liquid in which you have soaked the dried mushrooms, rather than the rehydrated mushrooms themselves.

Olive oil

I think that too much has been written about olive oil, but I am going to add to the existing mountain of words anyway. To my palate, the difference between decent but basic extra virgin olive oil and the stuff called just olive oil is enormous. I think that the latter item is not worth buying – if you want a neutrally flavoured oil, use sunflower oil, which is much cheaper.

However, the difference in taste between a decent but ordinary extra virgin olive oil, such as the Greek kalamata oil that we use at the restaurant (which costs about £3 per litre/1¾ pints), and the fancier estate-bottled oils (which may cost up to £15 per litre or more) is less significant. As with more expensive wine, there are some very specific tastes available from the estate-bottled olive oils and it can be interesting to try them, but my recommendation is to find a good, basic extra virgin oil that you like and forget the fancy stuff, except when you are in the mood for extravagant experimentation. If you do buy one of the more individual oils, only use it in dressings – the more subtle aromas would be completely lost in the cooking process.

Pulses – dried and tinned

It is occasionally said that one of the terribly difficult things about vegetarian cooking is that you have to remember to soak beans the day before you want to use them. There is a little truth in this; we don't always want to plan what we are going to eat a day in advance. It is partly, however, just a matter of habit. After all, it doesn't actually take very long to put a few chickpeas in a bowl and cover them with water.

It is also worth remembering that quite a few pulses do not require soaking – for example, lentils (red, green and Puy), split peas (green and yellow), and mung beans.

Tinned ready-cooked pulses are, in many cases, quite good – definitely worth keeping in the larder for when you find you have forgotten to soak your own. The disadvantage is that you have no control over what they are cooked or stored in. For instance, some tinned flageolet beans we recently bought had sugar in their brine. The quality of tinned pulses also varies very considerably. I have eaten tinned chickpeas that are plump and tender and others that are crunchy and taste incompletely cooked. If in doubt, go for a well-known brand. I have found Sainsbury's own-label chickpeas to be particularly good.

Incidentally, if soaking your own chickpeas, soak them in very heavily salted water. This is contrary to the instruction generally given in cookbooks, but, in the case of this particular pulse, it makes them tastier and more tender. The salty soaking water should be rinsed from the soaked chickpeas and they should then be boiled in fresh unsalted water. This tip came to me from a Greek Cypriot – and they know a thing or two about chickpeas in that part of the world. Also, the cooking liquor from chickpeas is always worth keeping for use in soups.

Soy sauce

Good-quality soy sauce is an excellent seasoning for a wide variety of food.

I recommend that you buy soy sauce from a healthfood shop rather than a super-market, as many brands sold in supermarkets do not taste so nice and are not made using traditional methods. The kind we use at The Place Below is called shoyu, but the alternative and equally good kind is tamari. Both are what are termed 'dark' soy sauces, and quantities given in this book are for this type of condiment, which is very strongly and deliciously flavoured.

Spices

The flavours of cumin and coriander are heightened when whole seeds are used and they are toasted (either in a pan, under the grill or in the oven) and ground just before using.

Nutmeg is much nicer freshly grated than ready ground, and you can buy excellent little nutmeg graters for this purpose.

Beware when preparing fresh chillies if you are not used to doing this. The juices from the chilli and its seeds can be highly irritating to skin, and especially eyes. Prepare onions before chillies so you don't rub chilli into your eyes. Gentlemen – make sure you have had a pee before preparing your chillies.

If you like less heat in a dish, discard the seeds, which are the hottest bit of the chilli.

Stock

None of the recipes assume that you either make or buy vegetable stock and neither do they necessitate the use of stock powder. The listed ingredients provide ample flavour. If you have freshly made stock to hand, use it as appropriate. I do not in general recommend the use of stock powder, which tends to give all soups a similar taste.

Tofu

Do not skip this entry! If you are one of the millions of people who think that tofu is inevitably disgusting, immediately turn to pages 127–8 and make the Roast Marinated Tofu or to page 125 and try the Rich Dill Dressing.

These two recipes each use one of the two easily available kinds of tofu. If you want chunks of tofu (which I personally never now eat without marinating and roasting), you need to use a firm tofu. This is easily available in supermarkets. For mayonnaise-type sauces, you need silken tofu, which has a much softer texture, and you can find this kind in healthfood shops.

You can also buy freshly made tofu at specialist Chinese grocery shops. It is undoubtedly a more authentic product, but, I have to confess, I have found it difficult to work with. It generally has a texture somewhere between firm and silken tofu.

Tomatoes

Tomatoes are a vital ingredient in a lot of vegetarian food. The best tomatoes for cooking are plum tomatoes, which have a low acidity, good flavour and a large proportion of flesh to seeds and juice. If this were a cookbook based on the fantasy that we all live in Tuscan farmhouses, I would say never use anything but fresh plum tomatoes. However, in the real world, for much of the year, it is not possible to get ripe, fresh plum tomatoes, and even if you can find them the price is often prohibitive.

The sensible answer is to use good-quality tinned plum tomatoes, which make excellent tomato-based sauces. It is tempting to substitute tinned, chopped tomatoes or other tinned tomatoes that do not specify they are plum tomatoes. Do not be tempted. We have experimented with all kinds of tinned tomatoes and tinned, whole, plum tomatoes are the best.

While testing these recipes in Cornwall, I also compared the most well-known and widely available brand of tinned plum tomatoes, Napolina, with various supermarkets' incredibly cheap own-label products. The Napolina tomatoes did seem to have a slightly better flavour and colour, although, admittedly, the test was done on a statistically insignificant number of tins.

For using in salads, my favourite is the French Marmande (not easily available in the UK, but worth seeking out). In their season, Gardener's Delight cherry tomatoes are also delicious. Sarah's dad, Jim, grows both these varieties in his garden in Kent, but, quite unreasonably, hasn't yet agreed to expand his operation to a size that would mean he could supply all the restaurant's needs.

The hard, pale-coloured products known as 'salad tomatoes' are not worth buying. If they are all that is available, have something else in your salad.

Measurements

Teaspoon and tablespoon quantities are calculated using proper measuring spoons and filling them until they are level.

As always, don't mix metric and imperial measurements in the same recipe.

Quantities of vegetables and olive oil in recipes in this book

If you are used to buying mushrooms by the 100 g (¼ lb) and peppers one at a time, you may find the quantities demanded for some recipes daunting, but try not to take short cuts. I've tried to make it clear in individual recipes where it's absolutely essential not to skimp on an individual ingredient, but, throughout, it's true to say that the quantities are there for a reason – it won't taste so good with less.

Similarly with olive oil. If you have a low-fat approach to cooking, you may find the recommended quantities of olive oil in this book hard to take. Before you reject the quantities out of hand try, for instance, the ratatouille recipe exactly as it is written. It really tastes much nicer made with the recommended amount of oil.

Eggs

All the recipes that need eggs require size 3 eggs unless it is stated otherwise in the ingredients list.

Vegans

Many of the recipes are suitable for vegans although I have not specifically highlighted them. If you are a vegan, you will not have any difficulty homing in on the appropriate recipes. If you have a vegan coming to supper and don't know exactly what to offer them, you can try any recipe in this book except those containing dairy products (milk, butter, cream, cheese), eggs, or honey. Chapters 2, 3 and 7 are all rich in recipes suitable for vegans.

Tin and baking dish sizes

I have tried to use as few different sizes of tins as possible in this book. Quiche and sweet tart recipes are all written for 23-cm (9-in) diameter loose-bottomed tins. Recipes requiring spring-release tins are also written for a 23-cm (9-in) size.

Bread and terrine recipes are written for 900-g (2-lb) loaf tins – except the brioche recipe, which works better in a 450-g (1-lb) tin.

Lasagne, filo pies, gratins and so on require a deep 23 by 33-cm (9 by 13-in) baking dish.

Some Menus

I really enjoy the process of thinking about what kinds of foods go well together on different occasions and in different seasons. Here are a few suggestions as to how you might combine some of the different ideas in this book – they include only a small proportion of the recipes in the book and are only there as a pointer. There is no need to try and follow any of these menus rigidly, although I must say that they all make me feel hungry.

I hope that you find all these menus attractively simple. We do also cook rather more elaborate food for private dinners (weddings, birthdays, anniversaries), but I couldn't fit it all into one cookbook, so I'm afraid you'll have to wait for the next one!

A Spring Supper

Place Below Daily Bread
Roquefort Terrine with melon and young spinach
Tagliatelle with Asparagus and Tarragon
Rhubarb and Strawberry Compote

Summer Dinner

Fresh Herb and Olive Oil Bread with Basil
Courgette and Feta Filo Pie with Patatas Bravas à la Place Below and green leaf salad
Summer Pudding

Autumn Supper

Butternut Squash and Basil Soup
Guinness and Mushroom Casserole with Smoked Cheddar Mashed Potatoes
and Savoy Cabbage
Chocolate and Prune Tart

Winter Lunch

Lentil, Roast Garlic and Lime Soup
Potato, Onion and Gruyère Gratin with Slow-cooked Red Cabbage
Apple and Pear and Almond Crumble

Winter Dinner

Scrambled Duck Eggs on Field Mushrooms
Roast Aubergine and Puy Lentils with Balsamic Vinegar and Cream
Pepperonata and Stilton
Celeriac and Potato Mash
Brioche, Orange and Marmalade Pudding

CHAPTER 1

Bread and Buns

Place Below Daily Bread

Celebration Breads:
Garlic and Olive
Sun-dried Tomato

Fresh Herb and Olive Oil Bread
Basil
Thyme

Brioche

Saffron Buns

Place Below Daily Bread

Our bread is at the centre of everything that we make. It is very simple, but has a beautifully balanced flavour. With its combination of wholemeal and strong white flour, it typifies our approach – we want to make food that tastes delicious even if it is not politically correct. When we first opened, we made a Granary-type loaf with a flour that had malted grains in it. One day, we ran out of the Granary flour and Ian experimented with this combination instead. We have made it like this every day since then.

At home, I often make bread in the evenings while cooking supper or generally messing about in the kitchen; it doesn't add very much time in the kitchen at all. Take it out just before going to bed and you're set up for breakfast, packed lunches, picnics . . .

If you want a quick and delicious supper snack, pinch a bit of dough at the end of its first rising and you've got a ready-made pizza base. See pages 62–5 for some ideas for scrumptious toppings.

MAKES TWO 900-G (2-LB) LOAVES

570 g (1¼ lbs) plain wholemeal flour
570 g (1¼ lbs) strong white bread flour
25 g (1 oz) soya flour (if you haven't got any soya flour,
add an extra 25 g / 1 oz of the other flours to
keep the same proportion of wet and dry ingredients)
700 ml (1¼ pints) lukewarm water (you may need a little more)
25 g (1 oz) sunflower seeds
25 g (1 oz) sesame seeds
4 tsp salt
2 sachets easy-blend yeast
2 tbsp sunflower oil

1) Put all the ingredients into a mixing bowl. Mix initially in the bowl with a large metal spoon, then tip the dough on to a clean worksurface and knead by hand for about 10 minutes. I usually use one hand only for kneading, if only because the phone invariably rings at the stickiest stage of the process. (At the restaurant, the kneading is all done by machine, but I have found that domestic dough hook attachments do not produce such a good result with this kind of dough, although they are essential for making a really rich brioche dough; see pages 19–20.)

2) Put the dough in a clean, large bowl and cover with clingfilm. Leave it in a warm place to rise for at least 30 minutes (beware of leaving it on top of an oven or Aga,

where the bottom of the dough may begin to cook). If the room is cool you will need to leave it for considerably longer. The dough is ready when it has roughly doubled in size.

3) Pre-heat the oven to 230°C/450°F/Gas 8. Grease two 900-g (2-lb) loaf tins with butter or solid vegetable fat (which seems to be more effective than oil).

4) Divide the dough in half. Shape each piece into a fat sausage with the seam at the bottom and place in the prepared tins. Allow to prove (rise for a second time) for 10 to 15 minutes (or twice that time if the room is cool). Just before they go in the oven, use a small, sharp knife to make a light cut lengthways along the tops of the loaves.

5) Place in the pre-heated oven and bake for 20 minutes. Turn down to 200°C/400°F/Gas 6 and bake for a further 20 minutes, until the loaves sound hollow when taken out of their tins and tapped on their bottoms. Leave to cool on a wire rack.

6) We use the same dough to make our rolls, for which we measure out the dough into 65-g (2½-oz) pieces and then shape. They take about 20 to 25 minutes to bake at 230°C/450°F/Gas 8.

Celebration Breads

When we are cooking for private parties – weddings, birthdays, anniversaries – we usually bake one or both of these special breads. They are almost too rich to be thought of as bread – more like a rolled-up pizza. Eaten warm with butter, they are so good it is easy to stuff yourself with so much that you have no room for anything else.

MAKES TWO 450-G (1-LB) LOAVES

½ quantity Place Below Daily Bread dough (see page 14)

GARLIC AND OLIVE FILLING

50 g (2 oz) butter (or vegan margarine if you want to keep it dairy free)
2 cloves of garlic, crushed
1 tbsp wholegrain mustard
1 tbsp dried oregano
50 g (2 oz) stoned olives, half puréed, half roughly chopped
Salt and freshly ground black pepper

SUN-DRIED TOMATO FILLING

100 g (4 oz) sun-dried tomatoes
50 ml (2 fl oz) olive oil
1 clove of garlic, crushed
¼ tsp Tabasco sauce
2 tsp balsamic vinegar

1) To make the garlic and olive filling, soften the butter and mix thoroughly with the other ingredients.

2) To make the sun-dried tomato filling, soak the sun-dried tomatoes in very hot water for 30 minutes, then drain. Chop the drained tomatoes very finely and mix with the other ingredients. (If you are using sun-dried tomatoes preserved in olive oil, then you can use them straight from the jar.)

3) To make 2 loaves of either bread, make the dough as given on page 14, following the method up until the end of the first rising.

4) Pre-heat the oven to 230°C/450°F/Gas 8. Grease a large baking sheet.

5) Knock the dough back and divide it in half. Using a rolling pin and a little flour to dust the pin and worksurface, roll one piece of dough into a rectangle measuring about 30 by 20 cm (12 by 8 in).

6) Spread half the filling on to the dough, starting at the nearest edge but leaving a border of about 2.5 cm (1 in) at each side and about 5 cm (2 in) at the far end. Starting from the end nearest to you, roll it up away from you like a Swiss roll, making sure that the seam ends up underneath the final sausage shape. To seal the two ends of the loaf, place the rolling pin at right angles to the loaf over each end in turn and press down quickly and firmly so it is flattened at the end. Tuck each flattened end under the loaf.

7) Repeat, using the remainder of the filling, with the second half of the dough.

8) Leave the loaves to prove (rise again) for about 15 minutes – longer if the room is cool. With a small, sharp knife, make 3 diagonal slashes along the top of each loaf, place apart on the greased baking sheet and bake in the pre-heated oven for 20 minutes. Then, turn down to 200°C/400°F/Gas 6 and bake for a further 10 minutes. The loaves are cooked when they are golden on top and sound hollow when tapped underneath. Leave to cool on a wire rack – you won't be able to wait until they are completely cold before tasting them, nor should you.

Fresh Herb and Olive Oil Bread

This is a delicious and rich bread in its own right, and is particularly good toasted as a base for antipasti. It is also the dough used underneath the Mushroom and Thyme Tart on page 61, and the Ratatouille and Gruyère Tart on page 60.

Fresh basil can be used instead of thyme, but then you will need a full bunch of basil as its flavour is not as strong as that of thyme.

MAKES ONE LARGE LOAF

½ bunch of thyme or 1 bunch of basil
450 g (1 lb) strong white bread flour
120 ml (4 fl oz) olive oil
1 sachet easy-blend yeast
2 tsp salt
275 ml (9 fl oz) warm water

1) Pull the leaves from the stalks of the thyme or basil and chop them roughly. Mix with the flour, oil, yeast and salt.

2) Add the warm water and mix well. Knead for about 10 minutes, adding a bit more flour if the dough becomes too sticky to knead.

3) Leave to rise for at least 2 hours (or up to 4 hours if the room is very cool), until the dough has doubled in size. It takes much longer to rise than normal bread dough because of the amount of olive oil in it.

4) Pre-heat the oven to 220°C/425°F/Gas 7. Grease a baking sheet.

5) Knock the dough back, shape it into a long sausage and place it on the prepared baking sheet. Allow to prove for between 30 minutes and 1 hour, then bake in the pre-heated oven for about 25 minutes, until the bread sounds hollow when tapped on its base.

Brioche

Brioche is one of my obsessions. Freshly baked brioche eaten with good strawberry jam and accompanied by a cup of strong but milky coffee is my idea of a good start to the day.

There are many different versions for the quantities of eggs and butter relative to flour. Anton Mosimann recommends using half the amount of butter given here, and Elizabeth David suggests about three quarters of the butter that we use. Our version is the most luxurious I have come across. The quantities are based on the recipe in the Roux brothers' excellent pâtisserie book, but the method is different.

I had more trouble adapting this recipe for home use than any other in the book, and I have come to the conclusion that an electric mixer with a dough hook is essential for making this recipe at home, unless you are a highly experienced and patient baker. The dough is so rich and sticky that kneading it by hand is a nightmare. If you do have such a machine, though, it is fairly straightforward, but it does take a very long time for the dough to rise (as it is so rich), so read through the recipe before starting and don't try it unless you are going to be around to put the loaves into the oven at the appropriate moment.

As well as being delicious as it is, when toasted it makes a wonderful base for savoury snacks – a sort of upmarket bruschetta. The last time I made it at home, we had a supper of two bits each of toasted brioche, one topped with mousserons (tiny wild mushrooms, available in the early summer) cooked with butter, garlic, wine and cream, and the other topped with steamed asparagus tossed in olive oil and lemon juice – yummy. It is also the best thing to use for our Brioche, Orange and Marmalade Pudding (see page 146).

MAKES TWO 450-G (1-LB) LOAVES OR ABOUT 7 INDIVIDUAL BRIOCHES

350 g (12 oz) strong white bread flour
50 ml (2 fl oz) milk
1½ tsp salt
1 sachet easy-blend yeast
4 size 4 eggs
25 g (1 oz) sugar
200 g (7 oz) butter, softened
1 egg yolk

1) You must start the dough the day before you want to eat the brioche. Put all the ingredients, except the butter and the egg yolk, into the bowl of the electric mixer. Mix briefly with a spoon to make a cohesive but slightly sticky dough, then put the dough hook on and knead on a low speed for 5 minutes.

2) Add one third of the softened butter and continue kneading by machine until the butter has been completely absorbed. Add the next third of the butter and repeat. Repeat once more with the final third of the butter. Once all the butter has been absorbed, continue kneading on a low speed for a further 10 minutes. The dough should be shiny and very soft. If your dough hook does not reach all parts of the bowl efficiently, you may need to stop the machine occasionally to scrape the dough away from those bits of the bowl not being reached. Once the kneading is done, cover the bowl with clingfilm and put in the fridge overnight.

3) The next day, prepare two 450-g (1-lb) loaf tins by thoroughly greasing them with butter. Take the dough from the fridge – it may have risen a little, a lot, or not at all, depending on the temperature of the room where you were kneading the day before and the temperature of the fridge. In any event, don't worry if it has not risen – it will do later, as long as the yeast wasn't past its sell-by date. Divide the dough in half and shape each piece into a fat sausage to fit into one of the tins. Leave to rise until the dough has at least doubled in size – which, be warned, will take 2 to 4 hours.

4) When the loaves look as though they are nearly ready, pre-heat the oven to 220°C/425°F/Gas 7. Brush the top of each loaf with the egg yolk, being careful not to get egg yolk on the tin, and bake them in the oven for 25 to 35 minutes, until the loaves sound hollow when they are taken out of their tins and tapped on the bottom. If after 25 minutes the loaves are not ready, turn the oven down to 190°C/375°F/Gas 5 and bake for 10 more minutes – this way the tops do not burn. Turn the loaves out and leave to cool on a wire rack.

5) The same method can be used for making individual brioches in the pretty, traditional, fluted brioche tins. We weigh the dough out for these individual brioches, using 90 g (3½ oz) for each. For the traditional appearance, you should separate off a little dough from each and roll it into a ball. You then put the rest of the dough into its tin, make a dent with your thumb in the top and sit the small ball you made in the dent. Brush with egg yolk to glaze and leave to rise as before. This recipe makes about 7 individual brioches.

Saffron Buns

During our three months' 'sabbatical' in Cornwall to prepare this book, we saw saffron buns for sale everywhere. They are rather like an exotic version of hot cross buns. This version is the business or, rather, as the Cornish phrase goes, the proper job. Made with real saffron and freshly ground coriander, the buns are guaranteed to spoil your appetite for dinner if eaten warm with butter and a drop of Cornish honey.

MAKES ABOUT 14 BUNS OR ONE 900-G (2-LB) LOAF

0.2 g saffron (half a standard spice jar)
2 tbsp warm water
450 g (1 lb) strong white bread flour
½ tsp salt
175 g (6 oz) unsalted butter, plus 25 g (1 oz)
75 g (3 oz) caster sugar
1 tsp coriander seeds, ground
225 g (8 oz) raisins
1 sachet easy-blend yeast
175 ml (6 fl oz) warm milk
25 g (1 oz) demerara sugar

1) Bake the saffron at 180°C/350°F/Gas 4 for 5 minutes, until the strands darken in colour. Whizz to a rough powder in a spice grinder and soak in the warm water for 1 hour.

2) Rub in, or whizz together in a blender, the flour, salt and first quantity of butter until the mixture forms even crumbs.

3) Add the rest of the ingredients, except the remaining butter and demerara sugar, mix together and knead for 10 minutes.

4) Leave to rise for about 4 hours (note that how long it takes depends on the warmth of the room; it can be as much as 10 hours in a cold one). The dough should have doubled in size at the end of the rising period. Like the brioche, this is a rich dough, so the rising is slow.

5) Divide the dough into about 14 pieces and form into balls. Lay out evenly on 2 or more greased baking sheets and allow to prove for 2 hours or until they have doubled in size. If making a loaf, grease a 900-g (2-lb) loaf tin, form the dough into a loaf, place in the tin and leave to prove for 2 hours or until it has doubled in size.

6) Pre-heat the oven to 190°C/375°F/Gas 5. Bake the buns for 20 minutes, until they sound hollow when tapped on the bottom. A loaf will need about 40 minutes at this temperature, then turn the oven down to 180°C/350°F/Gas 4 and bake for 15 to 20 more minutes.

7) Melt the remaining butter, take the buns or loaf out of the oven, brush with butter and sprinkle with the demerara sugar. Return to the oven for a couple of minutes. Leave to cool on a wire rack.

CHAPTER 2

Soups

Butternut Squash and Basil Soup

Lentil, Roast Garlic and Lime Soup

Butter Bean, Sage and Dill Broth

Mushroom and Tarragon Soup

Celeriac and Stilton Soup

Carrot and Tarragon Soup

Tomato, Saffron and Almond Soup

Green Minestrone

Spinach, Watercress and Green Pea Soup

Curried Parsnip Soup

Gazpacho

Butternut Squash and Basil Soup

This soup is a simple combination of two modern wonder ingredients – butternut squash and fresh basil – spiked with one of the most traditional wonder ingredients – fresh lemon juice. If you have never cooked with butternut squash, rush out and buy one at once. If you've ever thought that pumpkins and their squash relatives were nice to look at but boring to eat, this king of squashes will change your mind. It seems to be stocked year-round in some of the big supermarkets, but you may find locally grown butternut squash available in enterprising greengrocers from September to November.

Although it contains no butter, cream or milk, this soup has a deliciously rich and velvety texture and a lovely orange colour, flecked with green. Using the squash in this recipe, you only need to halve it lengthways, scoop out the seeds and chop it – peeling is not necessary.

SERVES 6

1 onion, chopped
50 ml (2 fl oz) olive oil
1 large butternut squash (about 900 g/2 lb), deseeded and chopped
1.2 litres (2 pints) water
1 bunch of basil, leaves picked off the stems
Salt and freshly ground black pepper
Juice of 1 lemon

1) Soften the onion in the olive oil.

2) Add the squash and sweat until it starts to go a bit mushy.

3) Add the water, bring to the boil, then turn down the heat and simmer for about 10 to 15 minutes, until everything is well cooked.

4) Add the basil; it does not need to be chopped. Whizz in a blender until smooth.

5) Season to taste with salt, freshly ground black pepper and lemon juice.

Lentil, Roast Garlic and Lime Soup

Just hearing the name of this soup makes me feel hungry. If you're ever faced with someone droning on about how you can't make a decent soup without chicken stock, tell them to go away and try this recipe. They'll smell how wrong they were before they can even get a spoon in to taste it.

If you're not familiar with the taste of roast garlic, it's also a demonstration of the wonderful versatility of this most magic of vegetables.

The olive oil whizzed in at the end adds an extra richness, but if you prefer a lighter taste, leave it out.

SERVES 6

2 good bulbs of garlic (around 16 good cloves)
350 g (12 oz) red lentils
1.5 litres (2½ pints) water
Zest and juice of 1 large or 2 small limes (it depends how much lime you like)
50 ml (2 fl oz) olive oil
Fresh coriander, to garnish (optional)

1) Pre-heat the oven to 220°C/425°F/Gas 7.

2) Separate the bulbs of garlic into their individual cloves, but do not peel them. Place them on a baking sheet in the oven for about 10 minutes. When the garlic is ready, it should give a little bit when you push it with your finger (be careful not to burn yourself), but there should still be a bit of resistance. (If you leave them to bake for too long, they will be very difficult and sticky to peel, and you will end up throwing away some of the innards with the skin.) Leave the garlic to cool, then peel it. Discard the skins and put the pulp on one side.

3) Place the lentils and water in a large pan. Bring to the boil and simmer until the lentils are thoroughly mushy.

4) Take the pan off the heat and add the lime zest, juice and garlic. Whizz either in a food processor or (much easier since you can leave it in the pan) with a hand-held blender. While you are whizzing, drizzle in the olive oil. It should disappear completely and not remain as a slick on the surface.

5) Season to taste and serve, garnished with a few leaves of fresh coriander, if using, for extra zing.

Butter Bean, Sage and Dill Broth

There is a superb bookshop just off the Portobello Road in London's Notting Hill called Books for Cooks. The range of cookbooks, current and old, British and foreign, there is, for anyone remotely interested in food, completely credit card boggling. In addition, they have a small kitchen, from which I have several times eaten the most delicious food. I first made this soup at The Place Below after eating something inspiringly similar at Books for Cooks.

This makes an extremely thick soup. Serve it with grated Parmesan and fresh bread with fruit to follow for a delicious lunch.

SERVES 6

175 g (6 oz) dried butter beans, soaked overnight
1.5 litres (2½ pints) water
2 cloves of garlic, crushed
175 g (6 oz) red onions, finely chopped
175 g (6 oz) leeks, finely chopped
175 g (6 oz) carrots, finely chopped
4 sticks of celery, finely chopped
50 ml (2 fl oz) olive oil
1 tsp salt
225 g (8 oz) ripe tomatoes, finely chopped, or
200 g (7 oz) tinned plum tomatoes, liquidized
1 tbsp soy sauce
20 fresh sage leaves, chopped
½ bunch of flat-leaf parsley, chopped
1 bunch of dill, chopped

1) Drain the soaking water from the butter beans and put them into a pan with the measured fresh water. Bring to the boil and boil fiercely for 10 minutes. Turn down the heat, cover and simmer for about 1 hour, until the butter beans are very tender (if they have begun to collapse, that is fine). Leave the beans in the pan in the cooking liquid.

2) In a large pan, sweat the garlic, onions, leeks, carrots and celery in the olive oil until tender, adding the salt part-way through the cooking. Add the butter beans, with their cooking liquid, the tomatoes and soy sauce. Bring back to the boil and simmer for about 15 minutes.

3) Just before serving, stir in the chopped fresh herbs and check the seasoning.

Mushroom and Tarragon Soup

There is a wonderful restaurant at a remote country house hotel in Herefordshire called Hope End. They grow a large proportion of the fruit and vegetables they use in an old walled garden just a few yards from the house. The food Patricia Hegarty cooks is a reflection of the excellent local and seasonal produce to which she has access.

After one visit there, I came back to The Place Below enthusing about a darkly rich and aromatic mushroom and tarragon soup I had eaten. This is the recipe Frances developed as a result and we now regularly serve.

Although, in most cases, fresh herbs are infinitely preferable to dried, the use of dried tarragon in a thoroughly cooked soup such as this seems to capture that herb's perfume very effectively.

SERVES 6

225 g (8 oz) onions, roughly chopped
2 tsp dried tarragon
50 g (2 oz) butter
1 tbsp plain white flour
1.2 litres (2 pints) water (you may need more)
225 g (8 oz) potatoes, roughly chopped
900 g (2 lbs) field mushrooms, roughly chopped
Salt and freshly ground black pepper
300 ml (½ pint) milk
150 ml (¼ pint) single or double cream
1 tbsp soy sauce

1) Cook the onions and tarragon in the butter until soft.

2) Add the flour and cook, stirring every now and again, for 1 to 2 minutes.

3) Add the water, potatoes, mushrooms and ½ teaspoon of salt. Bring to the boil, then turn down the heat and simmer until the potatoes are falling apart.

4) Add the milk, cream and soy sauce and blend using a hand-held blender or food processor. If you want a very smooth texture, blend in a goblet-type liquidizer, but mushrooms do not readily blend smoothly. Personally I'm perfectly happy with unblended bits of mushroom in the soup.

5) Season to taste and serve.

Celeriac and Stilton Soup

I'm still amazed at how often I meet people who, although in other respects happy and rounded personalities, do not regularly eat or cook with celeriac. Of course, I realize there may be a small minority who do not consider food and eating to be central to their existence, but there must be other explanations. Is it the warty and hairy look of the vegetable that daunts, its high price relative to other root vegetables or simply unfamiliarity?

We use it in several ways: mashed with potato as a superb mopper up of mushroomy gravies, in individual gateaux served with cranberry sauce, and in this soup. It is also much used in France in salads, grated. If this is done simply with olive oil and lemon juice it is lovely, but for me the classic celeriac remoulade, swathed in mayonnaise, is something to be avoided.

You should attack the celeriac with a large cook's knife, peeling the skin off thickly enough to get rid of all the bits of dirt and root hair that can go down the cracks and cavities. Unless you are going to cook it immediately, you should put cut pieces of celeriac into acidulated water (cook's jargon for water with a dash of lemon juice in it) as it goes brown quite quickly.

If you don't like Stilton, leave it out, add a little salt and you will have a delicious cream of celeriac soup.

SERVES 6

1 onion, roughly chopped
1 stick of celery, sliced
900 g (2 lbs) celeriac, peeled and cut into 2.5-cm (1-in) cubes
25 g (1 oz) butter
2 tsp plain flour
900 ml (1½ pints) water
300 ml (½ pint) milk
50 ml (2 fl oz) single cream
100 g (4 oz) ripe Stilton (optional – see above)
Freshly ground black pepper

1) Sweat the vegetables in the butter until the celeriac is very soft – at least 15 minutes.

2) Add the flour and cook it for 2 to 3 minutes, stirring occasionally.

3) Stir in the water, slowly at first, mixing it well with the flour, and bring to the boil. Simmer for 15 minutes.

4) Add the milk, cream and Stilton, if using, and reheat, but do not boil. Blend, then season with plenty of pepper (if using Stilton you probably won't need any salt).

5) If reheating this soup later, do not boil or the soup will separate.

Carrot and Tarragon Soup

The sweet herb and the sweet vegetable complement each other in this delicate soup. It does rely heavily on juicy, flavourful carrots, so don't bother making it if there aren't any nice ones available.

SERVES 6

50 g (2 oz) butter
50 ml (2 fl oz) sunflower oil
900 g (2 lbs) carrots, thinly sliced
1 large onion, roughly chopped
2 sticks of celery, finely sliced (or you'll get stringy bits)
2 tsp plain flour
2 tsp dried tarragon
1.2 litres (2 pints) water
Juice of 1 orange
Salt and freshly ground black pepper
120 ml (4 fl oz) single cream

1) Melt the butter and mix in the oil. Add the carrots, onion and celery and cook for at least 20 minutes, until extremely soft, to bring out the flavour.

2) Add the flour and tarragon and cook very slightly.

3) Add the water, stirring, bring to the boil and simmer for about 20 minutes.

4) Add the orange juice and blend. Season with salt and pepper. Add the cream, check the seasoning and reheat if necessary, being careful not to boil the soup, then serve.

Tomato, Saffron and Almond Soup

Cooking tradition is full of snobbery and prejudice. If it is expensive and rare, it must be delicious. I used to assume that saffron fell into the category of ingredients loved more for their expense than their taste, but I was wrong! I first really tasted it in a memorable risotto near Rome, and since then have used it in many dishes at The Place Below. The beautiful colour saffron produces is only half the story – its elusive, exotic aroma is what really sets my tastebuds going. There is no substitute. Try making this soup with saffron, then try it again substituting turmeric for the saffron. Or, better still, don't bother; take my word for it, saffron is delicious and, if used in combination with more humble ingredients, need not burst the bank.

Here saffron stars in Spanish-based combination with almonds and tomatoes. It gives a deep orange colour to tomato-based dishes. A thick version of this soup makes a lovely sauce for roasted spiced potatoes, parsnips and squash, and a close relative features in the casserole on pages 42–3.

If you have really ripe, fresh tomatoes available, then use them in this soup, but, being realistic, that is rarely the case in Britain. You will make a much nicer soup using decent-quality tinned plum tomatoes than unripe fresh tomatoes.

SERVES 6

2 cloves of garlic, crushed
1 large onion, roughly chopped
50 ml (2 fl oz) olive oil
2 x 400-g (14-oz) tins plum tomatoes
1.2 litres (2 pints) water
0.2 g saffron (half a standard spice jar)
100 g (4 oz) ground almonds
Salt and freshly ground black pepper
Soy sauce, to taste

1) Sweat the onions and garlic in the olive oil until soft.

2) Add the tomatoes, water (add a little less than the given quantity of water if you want a thick soup) and saffron. Bring to the boil, then simmer for about 30 minutes.

3) Add the ground almonds and cook the soup for 5 to 10 minutes more, until it thickens.

4) Blend, season to taste with salt, pepper and soy sauce and serve.

Green Minestrone

This is a herby version of minestrone in which the basil, mint and parsley combine with the split green peas to produce a fresh green sea in which the other vegetables float. This soup is not worth making unless you have fresh, decent-sized bunches of herbs – dried herbs will not do here. Try adding some asparagus and fresh green peas for extra luxury in the spring.

SERVES 6

175 g (6 oz) split green peas, boiled in plenty of water
1.2 litres (2 pints) water
2 cloves of garlic, crushed
350 g (12 oz) leeks, finely chopped
3 sticks of celery, finely sliced
50 ml (2 fl oz) olive oil
Salt and freshly ground black pepper
225 g (8 oz) potatoes, finely diced
175 g (6 oz) fine green beans, finely chopped
1 bunch of basil
1 bunch of mint
1 bunch of parsley
Juice of 1 lemon

1) Put the split green peas in a pan with the measured water. Bring to the boil and simmer until they are utterly mushy. Set on one side in their cooking liquid.

2) Sweat the garlic, leeks and celery in the oil until tender, adding some salt as you go.

3) Add the split peas and their cooking liquid and the potatoes. Continue cooking until the potatoes are tender.

4) Add the green beans and continue cooking until these are tender.

5) Pick the leaves of the herbs from their stalks and put in a blender with the lemon juice and whizz briefly. Add to the soup. Add more water if necessary to achieve the desired consistency. Season to taste and serve.

Spinach, Watercress and Green Pea Soup

The combination of spinach and watercress is an intensely green and earthy one, which I think is delicious.

SERVES 6

1.5 litres (2½ pints) water
100 g (4 oz) split green peas
2 cloves of garlic, crushed
2.5-cm (1-in) slice fresh ginger root, peeled and finely chopped
120 ml (4 fl oz) olive oil
450 g (1 lb) fresh spinach, roughly chopped
175 g (6 oz) watercress (2 good bunches)
Juice of 1 lemon
Salt and freshly ground black pepper

1) Put the water and split green peas in a large pan. Bring to the boil and simmer for about 1 hour, or until the peas are totally mushy.

2) Fry the garlic and ginger in half the olive oil in a large pan. After 1 minute, add the spinach and continue cooking for 5 minutes or so, until the spinach has completely collapsed.

3) Add the cooked peas with their cooking liquor and the watercress and bring back to the boil.

4) Take the pan off the heat, add the lemon juice, the remainder of the olive oil and blend thoroughly. Season well, check the consistency (you may need to add a little more water) and serve.

Curried Parsnip Soup

There seem to be a million and one versions of curried parsnip soup in existence, but probably most of them can be traced back to Jane Grigson's wonderful *Vegetable Book* (Penguin, 1980). The sweetness of parsnips marries beautifully with curry spices, and the butter and cream give a mouth-watering richness to this supposedly humble vegetable.

To make this soup taste as delicious as possible, first, use freshly roasted and ground cumin and coriander and, second, don't be tempted to take short cuts on sweating the parsnips – they should be really soft before you add the liquid, as this will give a much smoother texture to the finished soup.

Leaving the seeds in the chilli makes for a soup with a little fire as well as the aroma of curry, but if you prefer a milder taste, leave out the seeds or even leave out the chilli altogether.

SERVES 6

50 g (2 oz) unsalted butter
1 medium onion, chopped
1 clove of garlic, crushed
½ fresh chilli, finely chopped, with seeds
900 g (2 lbs) parsnips, peeled and roughly chopped
1 tbsp plain flour
2 tsp coriander seeds, toasted and ground
1 tsp cumin seeds, toasted and ground
1 tsp turmeric
1 tsp ground ginger
1.5 litres (2½ pints) water
450 g (1 lb) potatoes, peeled and roughly diced
150 ml (¼ pint) apple juice
Salt and freshly ground black pepper
150 ml (¼ pint) single cream

1) Melt the butter and cook the onion, garlic and chilli until the onion is soft.

2) Add the parsnips and, stirring occasionally, cook for 20 to 30 minutes, until the parsnips are really soft.

3) Add the flour and spices, mix well and cook for 2 minutes.

4) Add the water, potatoes, apple juice and 3 teaspoons salt, bring to the boil, then simmer for 20 to 30 minutes, until the potatoes are very soft.

5) Blend until smooth, then add the cream and season to taste with salt and pepper.

Gazpacho

I used to feel only moderate enthusiasm for gazpacho until Frances made this version. It is pure summer luxury – the richness of the olive oil and ground almonds balancing the attack of the raw vegetables. It is, incidentally, one of the few dishes where green peppers are a positive bonus, rather than being a cheap and inadequate substitute for red and yellow peppers.

This soup is much nicer if made the day before and chilled overnight so that the flavours have a chance to mingle. Tinned tomatoes are really no good for this soup as it is completely uncooked, so only make it if you can find some ripe, fresh tomatoes.

SERVES 6

225 g (8 oz lb) ripe tomatoes, roughly chopped
600 ml (1 pint) water
1 clove of garlic, crushed
2 tsp balsamic vinegar
120 ml (4 fl oz) olive oil
100 g (4 oz) ground almonds
1 cucumber, peeled and chopped
½ tsp Tabasco sauce
1 small onion, finely chopped
1 red pepper, deseeded and chopped
1 green pepper, deseeded and chopped
Salt and freshly ground black pepper
Juice of 1 lemon
1 bunch of flat-leaf parsley
1 bunch of mint

1) Put everything, except the parsley and mint, into a large bowl and blend with a hand blender (or a bit at a time in a food processor). Put in the fridge and leave overnight if possible.

2) Next day, chop the parsley and mint and stir into the Gazpacho just before serving.

CHAPTER 3

Casseroles

Guinness and Mushroom Casserole

Place Below Ratatouille

Butternut Squash, Pears and Chickpeas in a Saffron and Almond Sauce

Chilli Bean Casserole

Wild and Field Mushroom Ragoût

Spinach, Mung Bean and Lime Casserole

Boston Baked Beans

Mushrooms, Baby Corn and Sugar-snap Peas in a Satay Sauce

Field Mushroom, Puy Lentil and Fresh Thyme Casserole

Roast Aubergine and Puy Lentils with Balsamic Vinegar and Cream

Pepperonata with Stilton

Dal

Spinach and Potato Curry

Shallot, Fennel and Chestnut Casserole

Aubergine and Chickpea Harissa

Guinness and Mushroom Casserole

I am obsessed with food and wherever we go on holiday, I'm on the look-out for ideas and combinations that I can adapt for use in the restaurant. This is adapted from a dish we had on a windswept wintry night at Starlings Castle, a marvellous and remote restaurant with rooms on the Welsh border.

We have served it in two different ways – either with Roast Marinated Tofu (see pages 127–8) stirred in at the last moment and then accompanied by rice, or with Smoked Cheddar Mashed Potatoes (see page 105). This last makes one of my favourite fragrant and mouth-watering winter platefuls.

SERVES 6

2 cloves of garlic, crushed
2 medium leeks, halved, sliced and thoroughly washed
50 ml (2 fl oz) sunflower oil
225g (8 oz) swede, diced
225g (8 oz) carrots, diced
225g (8 oz) turnips, diced
900g (2 lb) field mushrooms, peeled and chunkily sliced
175 ml (6 fl oz) Guinness (drink the rest of the can)
225g (8 oz) tomatoes, finely diced, or half a 400-g (14-oz) tin, liquidized
2 sprigs of fresh or 1 tsp dried thyme
1 tsp molasses
2 tsp soy sauce

1) Fry the garlic and leeks in the oil in a large pan or casserole dish until the onions are transparent.

2) Add the swede, carrots and turnips and continue to cook with the lid on for about 10 minutes, stirring occasionally.

3) Add the mushrooms and continue cooking. At this stage, you will think that the recipe is wrong and has asked for too many mushrooms, but persevere. If your pan is not fairly large you may have to add the mushrooms half at a time and wait until the first lot have begun to shrink and give off their juices before adding the rest.

4) When the mushrooms have all begun to go soft, add the rest of the ingredients, stir well and simmer for about 15 minutes so the flavours mingle and the liquid begins to reduce.

5) At this point, the casserole will still be fairly liquid. You can serve it as it is, if you like to have lots of liquid to mop up with your rice or mashed potatoes – that's how I like it. If you prefer your gravy thicker, you can strain the liquid from the vegetables, put it in a separate pan, bring it to the boil and keep it at a rolling boil until the liquid has reduced by half, then add it back to the vegetables, reheat, check the seasoning and serve.

Place Below Ratatouille

Ratatouille can be the most delicious or the most insipid of dishes. It is easy to make it well, but, unfortunately, it is slightly quicker to make it badly. Follow our recipe and your eyes will be opened, but only if you are not tempted to either skimp on the olive oil or just to chuck everything in a pan and hope for the best.

We serve it in quite a few different ways. Traditionally it is served at room temperature and this probably brings out the rich mixture of flavours best, but in winter you may prefer it piping hot. Try it with bulgar wheat and fresh herbs and Haricot Bean and Roast Garlic Purée (see page 115), or with Special Mashed Potatoes with Pesto (see page 105). If you have any leftovers (unlikely!), use it as part of a pizza or to make a soup.

SERVES 6

1 large onion, halved and sliced
2 cloves of garlic
50 ml (2 fl oz) olive oil, plus 250 ml (8 fl oz) for roasting
2 x 400-g (14-oz) tins plum tomatoes
1 bunch of basil, roughly chopped
1 bunch of flat-leaf parsley, roughly chopped
Salt and freshly ground black pepper
750 g (1½ lbs) aubergines, chopped chunkily
2 red peppers, deseeded and chopped into eight lengthways
2 yellow peppers, deseeded and chopped into eight lengthways
450 g (1 lb) courgettes, sliced diagonally, not too thinly

1) Pre-heat the oven to 220°C/425°F/Gas 7.

2) First, make the sauce. Sweat the onion and garlic in the 60 ml (2 fl oz) of olive oil until the onions are very soft; this will take at least 15 minutes.

3) Add the tomatoes and bring to the boil. Simmer until the liquid has reduced by about a quarter. Take the pan off the heat, add the herbs and season to taste, then set on one side.

4) You will need 3 baking sheets for roasting the 3 different vegetables. With each of the vegetables to be roasted (aubergine, both types of pepper and the courgettes), place the vegetable in a large mixing bowl and toss it with sufficient of the remaining olive oil to coat the pieces without them becoming sodden. You will find that you use about two thirds of the oil on the aubergine and the remaining one third divided equally between the peppers and the courgettes. Season well and toss again. Lay out on the baking sheet (don't pile the pieces on top of each other) and place each tray in the pre-heated oven in the following order. The aubergines take longest to cook – about 30 minutes – so go in first. The flesh should be turning gold and they should have shrunk somewhat in size. Undercooking aubergines is why many people think they don't like the vegetable. The peppers go in about 10 minutes later as they will take about 20 minutes. They will just be turning black at the edge of the tray and the skins should be beginning to go wrinkly. Last, put the courgettes in about 10 minutes later. I like to leave the courgettes in for only about 10 minutes, so that they retain some of their crunch, but it is very much a matter of taste, and traditionalists will want them to have moved further towards a state of collapse than this.

5) Stir the roasted vegetables into the sauce, adjust the seasoning, reheat to the required temperature and serve.

Butternut Squash, Pears and Chickpeas in a Saffron and Almond Sauce

This is a recipe I have adapted from Annie Bell's excellent *Feast of Flavours* (Bantam, 1992) cookbook, and it appears regularly on our lunchtime menus. The method of thickening the saffron and tomato sauce with a picada, made from garlic and olive oil toast and ground almonds, was a real eye-opener for me. We usually serve it with bulgar wheat with parsley, mint and olive oil.

SERVES 6

175 g (6 oz) dried chickpeas

FOR THE PICADA

100 g (4 oz) bread, in thick slices
85 ml (3 fl oz) olive oil
2 cloves of garlic, crushed
50 g (2 oz) ground almonds, lightly toasted
1 tsp paprika
0.2 g saffron (half a standard spice jar)

FOR THE STEW

1 medium onion, chopped medium fine
2 tbsp olive oil
1 x 400-g (14-oz) tin plum tomatoes, liquidized
100 g (4 oz) carrots, sliced
100 g (4 oz) butternut squash, cubed (make lovely soup with the rest of the squash)
175 g (6 oz) French beans, cut in half
225 g (8 oz) unripe pears, cored and cubed
120 ml (4 fl oz) white wine

1) Soak the chickpeas overnight in heavily salted water.

2) The next day, drain the chickpeas and cook them in plenty of fresh, unsalted water until they are tender. Put on one side and keep the cooking liquid.

3) Pre-heat the oven to 220°C/425°F/Gas 7.

4) To make the picada, coat the slices of bread in the oil and crushed garlic and put them on a baking sheet. Bake in the pre-heated oven until golden.

5) Grind the toasts with the almonds in a blender until you have a smooth mixture. Mix in the paprika and saffron and you then have the picada.

6) For the stew, fry the onion in the olive oil until it is very soft.

7) Take the cooked chickpeas and their cooking liquid, drain off the liquid and make it up to 900 ml (1½ pints) with the wine and water. Add this to the onion and bring to the boil.

8) Add the vegetables and pears and cook for about 10 minutes, until all the vegetables are tender.

9) When the vegetables are cooked, add the picada and chickpeas, reheat, check the seasoning and serve. The sauce will continue to thicken if not eaten straightaway, so add a bit of extra water if necessary, but remember to recheck the seasoning.

Chilli Bean Casserole

Chilli is, of course, a classic veggie hippie stew, but this is a really delicious version, and is another product of Ian's days at Bart's restaurant and the Vegetarian Society's cookery school. Unlike the 'ironic chilli' recently spotted by Pseud's Corner at a retro 1970s dinner party, this is the real thing – as friendly as they come.

It is at its best served with Roast Sweet Potatoes (see page 110) and Guacamole with fresh coriander (see page 120).

SERVES 6

225 g (8 oz) dried red kidney beans
1 large onion, finely chopped
1 clove of garlic, crushed
½ small fresh red chilli, finely chopped with seeds
175 g (6 oz) carrots, halved and sliced
2 sticks of celery, sliced
1 green pepper, deseeded and diced
2 tbsp sunflower oil
1 tsp cumin seeds, toasted and ground
1 x 400-g (14-oz) tin tomatoes, roughly chopped
120 ml (4 fl oz) strong black coffee
Juice of 1 lemon
1 tsp white wine vinegar
1 tsp dried basil
Salt and freshly ground black pepper

1) Soak the kidney beans overnight.

2) The next day, drain the beans and put them in a large pan with plenty of fresh water. Bring to the boil and boil fiercely for no less than 10 minutes. Reduce the heat and simmer, covered, for at least another 40 minutes, until the beans are tender. Drain.

3) Sweat the onion, garlic, chilli, carrots, celery and green pepper in the sunflower oil until tender.

4) Add the cumin and cook for a further few minutes.

5) Add the remainder of the ingredients, including the kidney beans, and simmer for at least 30 more minutes.

6) Season to taste and serve.

Wild and Field Mushroom Ragoût

This is pure, rich mushroom flavour. Serve it with something plain – noodles, saffron rice, if you're feeling posh, or mashed potato for luxury comfort food.

Dried ceps are one of my all-time favourite ingredients. When feeling sad, I some-times take a jar out of the cupboard and sniff it for an instant high. I have eaten, cooked and picked fresh ceps, but I find the flavour of this wild mushroom more exciting dried than fresh. From a culinary point of view, the main thing is the liquor produced by soaking the dried mushrooms, rather than the reconstituted fungi themselves. The stock makes a superb risotto and a delicious clear sauce (watch out for the next book for recipes) and is an essential ingredient of this ragout. I buy the dried ceps in 500-g (1-lb) tubs even for home use, as buying the tiny packets they sell in supermarkets ends up being much more expensive. However, a little goes a long way – as you will taste the first time you use them.

You need a very large pot to cook this recipe, simply because mushrooms are extremely bulky before they cook down. If you don't have one, you may have to do the mushrooms in batches, but it's more of a hassle.

SERVES 6

50 g (2 oz) dried ceps
300 ml (½ pint) very hot water
2 large onions, sliced
2 cloves of garlic, crushed
50 g (2 oz) butter
900 g (2 lbs) field mushrooms, sliced
300 ml (10 fl oz) red wine
2 tbsp soy sauce
½ bunch of thyme, leaves stripped from the stalks
50 ml (2 fl oz) brandy
175 ml (6 fl oz) double cream (do not substitute single)

1) Soak the ceps in the hot water for at least 30 minutes.

2) Sweat the onions and garlic in the butter until soft.

3) Add the field mushrooms and continue cooking over a medium heat until the mushrooms are quite soft.

4) Drain the cooked mushroom mix thoroughly, collecting the juice in the pan in which you have been cooking them. Pick the ceps out of their soaking water and add them to the drained mushroom mix. Strain the soaking water through a fine sieve (to get rid of any grit) into the pan with the mushroom juice. Add the wine and soy sauce to the pan. Bring to the boil and continue to boil fiercely until it has reduced by half.

5) Add the brandy and cream and bring back to the boil. Simmer for a minute or so until the sauce begins to thicken. Add back the mushroom mix, reheat and check the seasoning before serving.

Spinach, Mung Bean and Lime Casserole

This is simple and delicious. I first ate it at Ian's restaurant, Bart's. The ingredients and flavours are simple but perfectly matched. Garlic, lime and beans is one of those combinations made in heaven, like tomatoes and basil.

The great advantage of mung beans is that, like lentils and split peas, but unlike most other pulses, you don't need to soak them.

Serve this dish with basmati or wholegrain rice.

SERVES 4–6

225 g (8 oz) dried mung beans
350 g (12 oz) onions, halved and sliced
3 cloves of garlic, crushed
2 tbsp sunflower oil
1 x 400-g (14-oz) tin plum tomatoes, chopped
450 g (1 lb) fresh spinach, washed and roughly chopped
Zest and juice of 2 limes
Salt and freshly ground black pepper
1 lime, to garnish

1) Boil the mung beans in plenty of water for about 45 minutes, until tender, then discard the cooking water.

2) Sweat the onions and garlic in the oil until soft.

3) Add the tomatoes and spinach, bring to the boil, then simmer for about 10 minutes, until the spinach is cooked.

4) Add the lime juice and zest. Check the seasoning, but note that, as with most pulse-based dishes, you will need to add plenty of salt.

5) Cut the remaining lime into 6 wedges and use to garnish each serving.

Boston Baked Beans

Authentic American recipes for Boston beans recommend that the dish is cooked for six to nine hours in a low oven. I suspect that this is as unrealistic for most cooks at home as it is in our intensively used ovens at The Place Below. It is also unnecessary. Nevertheless, slow cooking on top of the oven for at least one and a half hours is important to develop the rich and sweet mix of flavours fully. Tinned baked beans will never seem the same again – except, of course when prepared à la Bill (see page 121)!

Serve these Boston Baked beans with Roast Sweet Potatoes (page 110) and Cucumber, Apple and Mint Relish (page 121).

SERVES 4–6

225 g (8 oz) dried haricot or flageolet beans
50 ml (2 fl oz) sunflower oil
1 medium onion, finely chopped
1 stick of celery, finely chopped
225 g (8 oz) carrots, halved and sliced
2 tbsp molasses
4 tsp grainy mustard
50 ml (2 fl oz) soy sauce
1 tsp cumin seeds, toasted and ground
200 g (7 oz) tinned plum tomatoes, liquidized
85 ml (3 fl oz) Guinness

1) Soak the beans overnight.

2) The next day, drain the beans and cook in plenty of fresh water until tender. Drain.

3) Put all the ingredients, including the cooked beans in a heavy-bottomed casserole dish with a tightly fitting lid. Bring to the boil, stirring, then turn down the heat so the sauce is just bubbling, put the lid on and continue cooking over this low heat for at least 1 hour 30 minutes. Lift the lid and stir occasionally during this time and, if the beans are drying out, add a little water.

4) When the flavours have matured and all the vegetables are completely tender, check the seasoning and serve.

Mushrooms, Baby Corn
and Sugar-snap Peas in a Satay Sauce

The idea for this dish came from a meal we had at a staff Christmas party at someone else's restaurant. Our version (developed by Frances) is, of course, infinitely superior — well, I would say that, wouldn't I? At any rate, it sells better than virtually anything else on our lunchtime menu. The lemon grass, ginger, coconut and basil combination is a mouth-watering winner, which is presumably why it's used daily by millions of cooks in South-East Asia.

This is one of those recipes with an intimidatingly long list of ingredients, but don't let this put you off. It is, in fact, an easy dish to make — essentially blanched vegetables in a spiced sauce. Serve it with rice.

SERVES 4–6

225 g (8 oz) sugar-snap peas
225 g (8 oz) baby corn, whole
225 g (8 oz) carrots, sliced thickly
1 onion, chopped
2 cloves of garlic, crushed
½ fresh chilli, chopped
1-cm (½-in) slice fresh ginger root, peeled and chopped
1 stick of lemon grass, trimmed, outer skin removed and chopped
2 tbsp sunflower oil
2 tsp coriander seeds, toasted and ground
2 tsp cumin seeds, toasted and ground
2 tsp turmeric
1 x 400-ml (14-fl oz) tin coconut milk
150 ml (¼ pint) water
100 g (4 oz) peanut butter
Juice of 1 to 2 limes (only 1 if it is juicy)
Salt and freshly ground black pepper
225 g (8 oz) button mushrooms, halved
225 g (8 oz) beansprouts
1 bunch of basil, roughly chopped
100 g (4 oz) peanuts, tossed in salt and sunflower oil and roasted

1) Blanch the sugar-snaps, corn and carrots in boiling water, then drain, refresh in cold water and drain again.

2) Sweat the onion, garlic, chilli, ginger and lemon grass in the oil until soft.

3) Add the coriander, cumin and turmeric and cook for 1 to 2 minutes. Add the coconut milk and water, bring to the boil, then simmer for 15 minutes.

4) Take the pan off the heat and add the peanut butter and lime juice. Season to taste with salt and pepper.

5) Stir in the blanched vegetables, together with the mushrooms and beansprouts, and reheat until all the vegetables are hot. Stir in the basil and serve with the peanuts sprinkled over the top.

Field Mushroom,
Puy Lentil and Fresh Thyme Casserole

Anyone who is or has been a vegetarian will recognize the aggression that confessing to your eating preferences can bring out in otherwise calm individuals. Surely people can't feel threatened by their friends or family choosing to stick to a particular range of ingredients in their cooking and eating? One of the more absurd progressions of this conversation will be along the lines of, 'Of course, I don't/can't eat vegetarian, you see'. Ah, so you never have egg and chips, never beans on toast, never Welsh rarebit, never asparagus hollandaise? Why is it that otherwise sensible foodies, who have no difficulty accepting cuisines based on geographic (and therefore culinary) limitations (such as Thai food), have such difficulty accepting that there is a developing vegetarian cuisine based on a specific range of ingredients but without geographic limitations?

Forgive this outpouring of frustration. What I am trying to say is that this is a most delicious casserole to feed to those who think there is no natural flavour or satisfaction without meat. (In fact I've just realized, having reread this, that there are no dairy products either – better not mention that!)

Serve this dish with Celeriac and Potato Mash (see page 107).

SERVES 6

250 ml (8 fl oz) red wine
50 ml (2 fl oz) soy sauce
450 ml (¾ pint) water
225 g (8 oz) Puy lentils
2 cloves of garlic, crushed
1 large onion, halved and sliced
50 ml (2 fl oz) sunflower oil
1.25 kg (2½ lbs) field mushrooms, peeled and thickly sliced
1 bay leaf
100 g (4 oz) cashew nuts
1 bunch of thyme, leaves picked off the stalks, or 1 tsp dried thyme

1) Put the wine, soy sauce, water and lentils in a pot. Bring to the boil, then simmer for about 35 minutes, until the lentils are just tender. Set aside.

2) In a large casserole or heavy-bottomed pot, sweat the garlic and onion in the oil until soft.

3) Add the mushrooms and bay leaf (and the thyme if you are using dried). When the mushrooms are just going soft, add the lentils with their cooking liquor and remove the pot from the heat.

4) Whizz the cashews to a fine powder in a blender. While still whizzing, add the thyme (if using fresh leaves) and enough water to make a thick cream. Stir this mixture into the casserole, reheat, check the seasoning and serve.

Roast Aubergine and Puy Lentils
with Balsamic Vinegar and Cream

On a recent trip through France, Sarah and I found ourselves near Le Puy in the Massif Central. I rushed around buying an unnecessarily large number of packets of slate green Puy lentils, and was extremely excited to read of a local restaurant where the chef there described himself as 'The King of Lentils' (they're a modest lot, French chefs). Unfortunately, the restaurant was closed, but we did eat a delicious local salad described as *lentilles à l'àncienne*. The Puy lentils were dressed in a creamy but sharp emulsion and surrounded with crisp leaves. The following recipe evolved from those flavours, with the roast aubergine adding a contrasting velvety luxury. Incidentally, balsamic vinegar and cream also makes a delicious coating for Savoy cabbage.

Try serving this with some pepperonata (see page 54) and mashed potato.

SERVES 6

750 g (1½ lbs) aubergines, roughly diced
120 ml (4 fl oz) olive oil
Salt and freshly ground black pepper
225 g (8 oz) Puy lentils
2 medium onions, finely sliced
2 cloves of garlic, crushed
50 ml (2 fl oz) balsamic vinegar
1 tbsp soy sauce (or more to taste)
150 ml (5 fl oz) double cream
1 bunch of basil, finely chopped

1) Pre-heat the oven to 220°C/425°F/Gas 7.

2) Toss the aubergines in three quarters of the olive oil and season generously. Spread out on 2 baking sheets and roast in the pre-heated oven for about 30 minutes, until the white parts have turned golden and the flesh has begun to collapse.

3) While the aubergines are roasting, boil the lentils until they are just tender, but not collapsed (about 35 minutes), then drain.

4) Sweat the onions and garlic in the remainder of the olive oil until soft.

5) Add the cooked lentils and roasted aubergine to the onions. Stir in the vinegar, soy sauce and double cream. Reheat, check the seasoning, then stir in the basil, serve.

Pepperonata with Stilton

This may sound a weird combination, but I think it is a delicious one. Quite accidentally, the farm where we stayed in Cornwall while testing all these recipes was about a hundred yards from an unusually good pub called the Trengilly Wartha. The thought of the good food and beer so close often meant that fewer recipes were tested in a day than we had planned. One evening we had the Trengilly's chef and co-owner to dinner and served him this dish, together with Roast Aubergine and Puy Lentils with Balsamic Vinegar and Cream (see page 53) and some Celeriac and Potato Mash (see page 107) – yummy!

You can only make this dish on top of the stove if you have a really decent-sized pan as, to cook properly, all the peppers need to be in contact with the hot oil and onions at the bottom of the pan. If you do not have such a pan (I now carry one with me wherever I go – almost), then roast the peppers in the oven and stir them into the completed tomato sauce.

This is another recipe where you may feel frightened by the huge quantity of olive oil. Of course you can use less – it just won't taste so good.

You can make just a straight pepperonata without Stilton, but then you may want to season it more strongly.

SERVES 6 (AS PART OF A MAIN COURSE)

2 medium onions, halved and sliced
2 cloves of garlic, crushed
120 ml (4 fl oz) olive oil
3 red peppers, cut into strips
3 yellow peppers, cut into strips
1 x 400-g (14-oz) tin plum tomatoes, liquidized
1 bunch of parsley, chopped
100 g (4 oz) Stilton

1) Fry the onions and garlic in the oil until soft.

2) Add the peppers (see the note about pan size above) and cook, uncovered, over a low heat, stirring occasionally, for at least 30 minutes, until the peppers are soft.

3) Add the tomatoes and bring to the boil. Cover and simmer for about 20 minutes more.

4) Stir in the parsley and Stilton, check the seasoning and serve.

Dal

The first cookery book I owned was *The Vegetarian Epicure* by Anna Thomas (Penguin, 1973). I still think it is an excellent book – an enthusiastic affirmation of good and generous cooking and eating. One of the first things I cooked from it was the recipe for dal. When hiding from the appalling vegetarian food provided by my college, I used to feed it to my friends with rice and a strange-sounding, but very delicious, curry from the same book based on carrots, bananas and orange juice.

In India, every family has their own version of dal. Personally, I like it fragrant rather than fiery, well-salted and with plenty of butter or ghee. This delicious recipe owes something to Anna Thomas and something to our own Frances. Generally, in India, it has the consistency of soup, and that is how I like it, but simply add less water if you prefer it less sloppy. Indeed, it is delicious eaten as soup, or with Spinach and Potato Curry (see page 56), some rice and some chilli pickles.

SERVES 6 (AS PART OF A MAIN COURSE)

225 g (8 oz) red lentils
1.2 litres (2 pints) water
3 cloves
1 tsp coriander seeds, toasted and ground
1 tsp mustard seeds, toasted and ground
1 tsp cumin seeds, toasted and ground
1 tsp turmeric
½ tsp cinnamon
¼ tsp cayenne pepper
¼ tsp ground ginger
50 g (2 oz) butter
Salt and freshly ground black pepper

1) Boil the lentils in salted water with the cloves for about 20 minutes, until completely mushy.

2) Add the spices to the lentils and stir in the butter. Season to taste.

Spinach and Potato Curry

Spinach goes well with butter and spices, and so do potatoes. This curry was developed by Frances specifically to go with rice and dal. To complete the picture, get a couple of jars of Geeta's pickles – the garlic pickle and the chilli and lime are our favourites.

SERVES 6 (WITH RICE AND DAL)

3 cloves of garlic, crushed
350 g (12 oz) onions, sliced
150 g (5 oz) butter, melted
2 tbsp sunflower oil
750 g (1½ lbs) potatoes, halved and thickly sliced
1 tsp whole cumin seeds, plus 3 tsp toasted and ground
Salt and freshly ground black pepper
900 g (2 lbs) fresh spinach, washed
2 tsp coriander seeds, toasted and ground
1 tsp chilli powder

1) Pre-heat the oven to 220°C/425°F/Gas 7.

2) Sweat the garlic and onions in 75 g (3 oz) of the butter and the oil over a low heat for at least 40 minutes, until very soft.

3) Meanwhile, put the potatoes in a large pan in plenty of salted water. Bring to the boil, then simmer for a little under 10 minutes, until not quite cooked.

4) Drain and then toss in the remainder of the butter, the whole cumin seeds and some salt. Spread out in a roasting tin and bake in the pre-heated oven for about 1 hour, until crisp and golden on the outside and thoroughly tender inside. Turn the oven right down, then keep warm until you need them.

5) Put the spinach in a large pan with a tight-fitting lid over a low to medium heat. If it is still a bit wet from washing, it will cook in its own water, otherwise add a splash of water to the pan. Cook with the lid on for about 10 minutes, until the spinach is completely tender, then drain very thoroughly.

6) Add the drained spinach and the ground cumin, coriander and chilli powder to the garlic and onion. Cook over a low heat for about 15 minutes, so that the flavours mingle thoroughly. Season to taste. Stir in the cumin roast potatoes just before serving, so that they do not become soggy.

Shallot, Fennel and Chestnut Casserole

Sarah and I have been debating the virtues of chestnuts for years. She thinks they're great, I haven't been so sure. I made this dish to prove my point. As always, she was right – it's delicious. Tinned chestnuts are fine for this recipe.

Spicy roast potatoes and Savoy cabbage are good accompaniments for this dish.

SERVES 6

50 ml (2 fl oz) olive oil
450 g (1 lb) shallots, peeled and left whole
450 g (1 lb) fennel, roughly chopped
1 x 400-g (14-oz) tin plum tomatoes, liquidized
300 ml (½ pint) red wine
225 g (8 oz) tinned or vacuum-packed chestnuts
50 ml (2 fl oz) soy sauce
2 sprigs of fresh thyme
About 20 sage leaves, finely chopped
Salt and freshly ground black pepper

1) Heat the olive oil in a large casserole dish. Add whole shallots, and cook for about 20 minutes over a medium heat, until browned and becoming tender.

2) Add the fennel, stir, cover and cook for 10 minutes.

3) Add the remainder of the ingredients and bring to the boil. Simmer for 1 hour; the chestnuts should be almost falling apart.

4) Season to taste and serve.

Aubergine and Chickpea Harissa

Harissa is a spicy Moroccan paste, and it is useful to make it in slightly larger quantities than you need as you can then keep it in the fridge for a couple of weeks to add a spicy touch to unsuspecting food.

Both aubergines and chickpeas go well with spicy flavours, hence this combination. Serve it with couscous.

SERVES 4–6

225 g (8 oz) chickpeas, soaked overnight in heavily salted water
750 g (1½ lbs) aubergines, chunkily diced
120 ml (4 fl oz) olive oil
Salt and freshly ground black pepper
1 large onion, halved and sliced
1 x 400-g (14-oz) tin plum tomatoes, liquidized
225 g (8 oz) French beans, halved
2 level tbsp Harissa (see page 119)
1 bunch of coriander, to garnish

1) Make the Harissa as given on page 119 the day before.

2) Drain the soaked chickpeas and boil them in plenty of fresh water for about 50 minutes, until tender.

3) Pre-heat the oven to 220°C/425°F/Gas 7.

4) Toss the aubergines in three quarters of the olive oil and season generously. Spread them out on a couple of baking sheets and bake in the pre-heated oven for about 30 minutes, until golden on the outside and no longer chewy.

5) Sweat the onion in the remainder of the oil until soft.

6) Add the tomatoes, bring to the boil and simmer for about 30 minutes, adding the chickpeas about 15 minutes into this time.

7) Stir in the cooked aubergines and reheat. Then, stir in the Harissa a bit at a time until a reasonable level of fierceness is reached. Check the seasoning and serve, garnished with the fresh coriander.

CHAPTER 4

Pizza and Pastry Dishes

Ratatouille and Gruyère Tart

Mushroom and Thyme Tart

Onion and Parmesan Pizza

Sun-dried Tomato and Goats' Cheese Pizza with Roast Vegetables

Wholemeal Pastry for Quiches
Baking pastry cases blind

Leek and Gruyère Quiche

Roast Pepper and Goats' Cheese Quiche

Roast Potato, Red Onion and Smoked Cheddar Quiche

Ratatouille and Gruyère Tart

This is not the quickest recipe to make in this book, but it tastes wonderful and looks great, too. If you can get Gruyère off the wheel (cut from a large circular farmhouse cheese) it tastes much better than the kind cut from a long brick-like slab.

Both this and the Mushroom and Thyme Tart (see page 61) are half way between a quiche and a pizza as the dough is made with yeast but the topping is set with eggs. Should there be a new category of food known, perhaps, as quizza or puiche?

Serve this tart straight from the oven with a plain green salad.

SERVES 6, GENEROUSLY

½ quantity Fresh Herb and Olive Oil Bread dough made with basil (see page 18)
½ quantity Place Below Ratatouille (see pages 40–41)
3 eggs, lightly beaten
100 g (4 oz) Gruyère, grated

1) Make the bread dough as given in recipe on page 18, following the steps as far as the end of the first long rising.

2) Grease a 23-cm (9-in) spring-release tin. Shape the dough to fit the base of the tin and pull it about two thirds of the way up the sides. Allow to prove (rise for a second time at room temperature) for at least 20 minutes.

3) While the dough is rising, make the ratatouille as given on pages 40–41.

4) Pre-heat the oven to 190°C/375°F/Gas 5.

5) Stir in the eggs and Gruyère while the ratatouille is still hot so that it thickens a little. The base of the tart will not become soggy if the mixture is not too runny when it goes in.

6) Pour the ratatouille mix into the dough case. Bake in the pre-heated oven for about 50 minutes, until the topping is set and the dough cooked.

Mushroom and Thyme Tart

This is a recipe I developed while writing this book, when I discovered a shop selling Chanterelles and Pied de Mouton wild mushrooms. However, I have found that it is also delicious using a mixture of field and oyster mushrooms, both of which are more readily available. Do not use button mushrooms, as they do not have a strong enough flavour.

SERVES 6

½ quantity Fresh Herb and Olive Oil Bread dough made with thyme (see page 18)
900 g (2 lb) mixed mushrooms (see above) roughly chopped
120 ml (4 fl oz) olive oil
2 cloves of garlic, crushed
Salt and freshly ground black pepper
½ bunch of thyme, stalks discarded, leaves roughly chopped
120 ml (4 fl oz) white wine
120 ml (4 fl oz) double cream
2 eggs, beaten
100 g (4 oz) Parmesan

1) Make the bread dough as given in recipe on page 18, following the steps as far as the end of the first long rising.

2) Grease a 23-cm (9-in) spring-release tin. Shape the dough to fit the base of the tin and pull it about two thirds of the way up the sides. Allow to prove (rise for a second time) at room temperature for at least 20 minutes.

3) Pre-heat the oven to 190°C/375°F/Gas 5.

4) Fry the mushrooms in small batches in the oil with the garlic, salt, pepper and the remaining thyme. Lift the cooked mushrooms out of the pan and set to one side, keeping them warm.

5) Add the wine to the mushroom pan while still hot and reduce to half its volume. Add the cream and bring to the boil, then simmer for about 5 minutes.

6) Remove the pan from the heat and stir in the beaten eggs. Return it to the heat and stir continuously until the mixture just begins to thicken, then remove it from the heat and stir in the Parmesan and cooked mushrooms.

7) Pour the mixture into the tin lined with dough and bake in the pre-heated oven for 50 minutes, until the topping is just set and the dough is cooked.

Onion and Parmesan Pizza

As Elizabeth David points out in her fascinating book *English Bread and Yeast Cookery* (Penguin, 1979), pizzas were originally just a tasty Mediterranean way of using up leftover bits of dough in a bakery. They would be smeared with a bit of onion and tomato, or whatever was available and cheap.

I often make pizza at home when making bread. I just separate off a fistful of dough and cover it with bits of whatever I happen to have that will go together well – fresh or sun-dried tomatoes, mushrooms, onions, shallots, any cheese that will melt and be tasty, pesto, rosemary, oregano or basil. It is amazing what deliciousness can result from unplanned combinations.

This pizza is very much in that tradition, using only leftover bread dough and basic ingredients that I would aim always to have to hand. If starting from scratch I would probably use a white flour and olive oil dough (see Sun-dried Tomato and Goats' Cheese Pizza with Roast Vegetables, pages 64–5), but Place Below Daily Bread dough (see pages 14–15) makes a homely and tasty alternative.

The pizza is ready to eat straight from the oven. I think it is also delicious cold, but not everyone agrees with me.

SERVES 6

550 g (1¼ lbs) dough (*see above*)
3 large onions, halved and sliced
2 cloves of garlic, crushed
1 tsp dried oregano
Salt and freshly ground black pepper
120 ml (4 fl oz) olive oil
100 g (4 oz) black olives
90-g (3-oz) piece of Parmesan

1) Prepare the dough as given on pages 14–15 or 18, following the steps as far as the first rising.

2) Pre-heat the oven to 220°C/425°F/Gas 7.

3) Oil a 23 by 33-cm (9 by 13-in) baking sheet. Roll out the dough on to the sheet and allow to rise for 15 to 25 minutes, until it has doubled in thickness.

4) Meanwhile, sweat the onions, garlic and dried oregano in the olive oil over a medium to low heat for about 30 minutes, until very soft and sweet. Season well with salt and pepper.

5) Spread the cooked onions evenly over the pizza dough and decorate with the olives. (If you are using olives with the stones still in – and most nice olives do – make sure the people eating the pizza know!)

6) Bake in the pre-heated oven for 15 minutes.

7) Then, take it out and shave the Parmesan randomly over and return it to the oven for 5 more minutes, until the base is fully cooked. The best tool for making parmesan shavings is a U-shaped vegetable peeler. Also, if you put the Parmesan on the raw dough, it loses its delicious salty/sweet flavour.

Sun-dried Tomato and
Goats' Cheese Pizza with Roast Vegetables

This is a slightly more elaborate dish than the Onion and Parmesan Pizza (see pages 62–3), combining sun-dried tomatoes, roast peppers, courgettes and aubergine, and goats' cheese. They make an excellent pizza. You can either make a large one, as described below, or, for a smarter presentation, make individual round or oval pizzas.

SERVES 6

FOR THE PIZZA DOUGH

400 g (14 oz) strong white bread flour
250 ml (8 fl oz) lukewarm water
50 ml (2 fl oz) olive oil
1 tsp salt
1 sachet easy-blend yeast

FOR THE TOPPING

1 large aubergine, roughly chopped
120 ml (4 fl oz) olive oil
Salt and freshly ground black pepper
3 peppers, red and yellow, deseeded and cut into strips
450 g (1 lb) courgettes, thickly sliced diagonally
175 g (6 oz) mature goats' cheese, sliced

FOR THE SUN-DRIED TOMATO SAUCE

1 clove of garlic, crushed
2 tsp balsamic vinegar
100g (4 oz) sun-dried tomatoes in oil
50 ml (2 fl oz) oil, from the sun-dried tomatoes

1) Pre-heat the oven to 220°C/425°F/Gas 7.

2) Put all the ingredients for the dough in a bowl. Knead for about 10 minutes. Put back in the bowl and cover it with clingfilm. Leave to rise for at least 30 minutes, until it has doubled in size.

3) Meanwhile, make the topping. Toss the aubergines in half the olive oil and season with plenty of salt and pepper. Put on a baking sheet and roast in the pre-heated oven for about 30 minutes, until turning golden and soft. Toss the peppers in half the remaining olive oil and, again, season generously. Put on a baking sheet and roast for about 20 minutes, until the peppers are just beginning to colour at the edges. Toss the courgettes in the remaining olive oil and season, but do not roast.

4) While the aubergines and peppers are roasting, make the sun-dried tomato sauce. Put the garlic, vinegar and tomatoes in a food processor and whizz for a few seconds. While still whizzing, pour in the oil from the tomatoes and whizz until smooth.

5) When the dough has risen, knock it back and roll it out onto an oiled baking sheet measuring about 33 by 23 cm (13 by 9 in). Allow the dough to rise again for about 15 minutes, until it has doubled in thickness. Spread the sun-dried tomato sauce evenly over it. Arrange the aubergines and then the peppers on top, and then the dressed but uncooked courgettes on top of that. Last, arrange the slices of goats' cheese on top.

6) Bake in the pre-heated oven for 30 minutes, until the dough is completely cooked and the cheese is bubbling and golden.

Wholemeal Pastry for Quiches

This is very easy to make, but the really good thing is that it's incredibly easy to work with and produces thin and tasty wholemeal pastry. *Time Out* has twice described our quiches as the best in London, and one important factor in their success is this pastry recipe, which – like many good things – came to us from Ian's former restaurant in Surrey.

If you're convinced that wholemeal pastry is inevitably thick, solid and unappetizing, just suspend your judgement until you taste your first Leek and Gruyère Quiche (see page 68) or, in fact, anything else you make with this recipe.

Making pastry is a kind of basic housekeeping task in the kitchen – you don't want to have to do it more often than necessary. (Is that a very unwholesome view of housekeeping?) The quantities given here are sufficient to make two 30-cm (12-in) or three 23-cm (9-in) quiches, though all the recipes for quiches and tarts in this book are for the 23-cm (9-in) size.

Remember to use a vegan margarine rather than butter if you are going to use any of the pastry for a vegan dish.

MAKES TWO 30-CM (12-IN) OR THREE 23-CM (9-IN) PASTRY CASES

350 g (12 oz) plain wholemeal flour
175 g (6 oz) butter or hard vegan margarine
100 ml (3½ fl oz) water
40 ml (1½ fl oz) sunflower oil

1) Put the flour and butter or hard margarine into a blender. Whizz briefly – a couple of times should do it – until the mixture resembles breadcrumbs. You should not be able to see any separate bits of fat.

2) Leaving the machine going, pour in both the water and oil at once. The mixture should come together into a ball quite quickly. Stop the machine at this point. If you are used to making pastry, particularly white pastry, you may think that the mixture is too wet, but it isn't. The bran in the wholemeal flour will continue to absorb water as the dough rests.

3) Divide the pastry into the number of pastry cases you are going to make and wrap each ball of dough in clingfilm. Any you are going to use in the next day or two put in the fridge, while the rest can go in the freezer.

4) Even if the pastry is for immediate use, it must cool down and rest in the fridge for at least 1 hour, preferably longer. Do not try to roll it out immediately after making it, as you will have a nasty mess on your hands!

Baking pastry cases blind

If you are used to rolling out and baking pastry blind, ignore this page.

1) Pre-heat the oven to 220°C/425°F/Gas 7.

2) Take one of your balls of pastry out of the fridge. If it is very hard, knead it slightly before beginning to roll it out. Shape it into a small, flat disc.

3) Lightly dust your worksurface and rolling pin with flour. Rolling away from you, roll the pastry once, then turn the pastry through 45 degrees. Repeat, turning in the same direction until you have a circle about 5 cm (2 in) larger in diameter than your quiche tin.

4) Roll the pastry around your rolling pin to lift it over the tin, then gently unroll it on to the tin. Press it well into the base of the sides, feeding more pastry in from above in order to do this, to avoid stretching the pastry (if you stretch it at this point, it will shrink when baked and you will be left with a very low-sided tart or quiche). Press the pastry firmly against the sides. Cut it off at the top by running your hand round the top to give a neat edge.

5) Prick the base all over with a fork and bake in the pre-heated oven for 10 to 12 minutes, until the pastry is just turning golden at the edges. A sweet pastry, like that in the Tarts and Puddings chapter, will take nearer 10 minutes, while the wholemeal will take more like 12.

6) Lots of people recommend using beans to stop the pastry rising in bubbles in the middle of the base. However, we have found that, provided the base is thoroughly pricked over and the pastry has not been stretched, this is not necessary.

7) When baking sweet pastry blind (see page 147), you may need to put a second tart tin of the same size inside the pastry case to stop the sides collapsing, but only if you are using a deep tin. All the recipes in this book are written for a shallow tin, so you will only need to do this if you are using the sweet pastry for your own recipes.

Leek and Gruyère Quiche

Of all the quiches we make, this is the most popular. Leek, Gruyère and mustard is one of those combinations made in heaven, and we also use a richer version as a filling for individual brioches. As with all quiches, it is important to season the vegetables well before mixing them with the rest of the ingredients.

A note regarding cleaning leeks. They can have bits of dirt in the most peculiar places. The best way to clean them thoroughly is to halve them lengthways, leaving only the very base of the leek intact, chop them thoroughly and put the pieces in a large basin of clean water. Swish them around and the pieces of leek will float to the top and the dirt will sink to the bottom. Scoop the leek pieces off the top and put in a colander to drain.

SERVES 4–6

1 x 23-cm (9-in) wholemeal pastry case, baked blind (*see pages 66–7*)
450 g (1 lb) leeks, halved and finely chopped, including green parts
2 tbsp sunflower oil
Salt and freshly ground black pepper
100 g (4 oz) Gruyère, grated
250 ml (8 fl oz) single cream
2 eggs, beaten
1 tbsp grainy mustard

1) Pre-heat the oven to 190°C/375°F/Gas 5.

2) Sweat the leeks in the oil until tender. Season well with salt and pepper, drain and reserve any juice for soup.

3) Mix the rest of the ingredients together thoroughly and stir into the leeks. Spoon this mixture into the pastry case.

4) Bake in the pre-heated oven for about 30 to 40 minutes, until the filling has set. Allow it to sit for 5 minutes after it comes out of the oven and it will slice more easily. Best eaten hot.

Roast Pepper and Goats' Cheese Quiche

The sweet taste of roast peppers marries beautifully with the pungency of mature goats' cheese. A salad of mixed leaves and roast peppers topped with a briefly grilled individual Rocamadour goats' cheese makes a delicious starter and a similar combination works well in this more substantial quiche.

You need to find a mature goats' cheese log for this dish and there are plenty of good varieties available, both British and French. Do not use a fresh goats' cheese – the light creaminess of something like a Rosary goats' cheese is delicious uncooked in a salad, but does not work in cooking. You want the kind with a rind, which is often presented wrapped in straw.

We also add a bit of grated Cheddar to the mixture so that you don't have a bland, eggy custard between the bits of roast pepper and goats' cheese. The quiche looks prettiest if you use a mixture of red and yellow peppers. Do not use green peppers, though, as the taste is too bitter.

SERVES 6

1 x 23-cm (9-in) wholemeal pastry case, baked blind (see pages 66–7)
1 lb (450 g) red and/or yellow peppers, deseeded and sliced into 1-cm (½-in) wide strips.
50 ml (2 fl oz) olive oil
Salt and freshly ground black pepper
2 eggs, lightly beaten
150 ml (¼ pint) single cream
50 g (2 oz) Cheddar, grated
100 g (4 oz) mature goats' cheese log

1) Pre-heat the oven to 220°C/425°F/Gas 7.

2) Put the peppers and olive oil in a roasting tin and season well. Bake in the pre-heated oven for about 20 minutes, until the peppers are just colouring at the edges and beginning to lose their firmness. Set the cooked peppers aside and turn the oven down to 190°C/375°F/Gas 5.

3) Mix together the eggs, cream and Cheddar and season with a little salt and pepper. Scatter the roast peppers randomly in the pastry case, pour the egg mixture over them, then cut the goats' cheese into 6 slices and lay them around in a circle.

4) Bake the quiche in the pre-heated oven for about 30 minutes, until the filling has set and is just turning golden on top. When serving, cut it so that each person gets a round of goats' cheese.

Roast Potato,
Red Onion and Smoked Cheddar Quiche

Potatoes, onions and cheese – all three are high on my list of the world's most delicious things. And when the potatoes are roasted, the onions are red and sweetly caramelized and the Cheddar is smoked, you know you're on to a winner.

SERVES 4–6

1 x 23-cm (9-in) wholemeal pastry case, baked blind (see pages 66–7)
1 medium potato, unpeeled and diced
2 red onions, peeled and each cut into 8 segments
50 ml (2 fl oz) olive oil
Salt and freshly ground black pepper
150 ml (¼ pint) single cream
2 eggs, lightly beaten
100 g (4 oz) smoked Cheddar, grated

1) Pre-heat the oven to 220°C/425°F/Gas 7.

2) Bring a small pan of water to the boil, put the diced potato in it and simmer for 5 minutes, then drain.

3) Put the blanched potato and the red onion segments in a roasting tin, toss with the olive oil and season with salt and pepper. Bake in the pre-heated oven for about 25 minutes, until the onions are coloured on the outside and soft in the middle and the potatoes are crisp. Turn the oven down to 190°C/375°F/Gas 5.

4) In a large bowl, combine the cream, eggs, cheese and a little salt and mix together thoroughly. Stir in the roast potatoes and onions and pour everything into the pre-baked pastry case.

5) Bake for about 30 minutes, until the filling has set and is just beginning to turn golden on top.

CHAPTER 5

Pasta

Tagliatelle with Courgettes, Pecorino and Capers

The idea for this combination of flavours came from a wonderful dish Shaun Hill used to make at Gidleigh Park.

It is not always easy to find good aged Pecorino. If you are in London, one of the best places to go is Fratelli Camisa in Soho. You can substitute good Parmesan, but the flavour of the Pecorino, which is a sheep's cheese, is quite distinct. The Pecorino in supermarkets is unlikely to be mature enough, so if that's all you can find, substitute Parmesan.

SERVES 6

1 onion, roughly chopped
150 ml (¼ pint) olive oil
450 g (1 lb) fresh plum tomatoes, chopped, or
1 x 450-g (1-lb) tin chopped plum tomatoes
1 clove of garlic
1 packet silken tofu
Salt and freshly ground black pepper
450 g (1 lb) dried tagliatelle
450 g (1lb) courgettes, halved and sliced
50 g (2 oz) capers, drained
50 g (2 oz) stoned black olives, drained and chopped in half
225 g (8 oz) aged Pecorino or Parmesan, finely grated

1) Sweat the onion until soft in 2 tablespoons of the olive oil until soft.

2) Add the tomatoes and cook until you have a thick sauce. Put in a blender and whizz. While still whizzing add the garlic and tofu, whizz till smooth. Then, still whizzing, gradually add most of the rest of the olive oil (reserving a little to fry the courgettes).

3) Put on a large pan of salted water to boil. When it is boiling, add the tagliatelle.

4) At the same time, heat the remaining olive oil in another pan and fry the courgettes on a high heat, stirring continuously. Season with salt and pepper. They are done when they are just colouring on both sides.

5) As soon as the pasta is cooked, drain it and put it in the pan with the courgettes. Add the sauce, capers, olives and half the Pecorino or Parmesan and stir together quickly. Check the seasoning and serve at once. Serve the rest of the cheese in a bowl.

Pasta with Broccoli, Pesto and Cherry Tomatoes

When pesto first started appearing on restaurant menus a few years ago, chefs played with it like a new toy – mint pesto, coriander pesto, pesto with different cheeses or no cheese at all, walnuts instead of pine nuts. We too, regularly had a dish on the menu of mint pesto with baby vegetables and new potatoes. It was very nice, but I've gradually come round to the feeling that there is nothing to beat traditional basil pesto, and it cries out to be married with starch – pasta being the most obvious example, although it also does its magic with bread dough in pizza or loaves and with mashed potato.

Here the unctuousness of the pesto is balanced by the cherry tomatoes and deliciously mopped up by the broccoli florets. The colours are also gorgeous.

SERVES 4, GENEROUSLY

175 g (6 oz) Pesto (see pages 117–18)
350 g (12 oz) dried pasta, such as penne
350 g (12 oz) cherry tomatoes, halved
225 g (8 oz) broccoli, divided into florets

1) Make the Pesto as given on pages 117–18.

2) Put plenty of salted water in a large pan and bring to the boil. Add the pasta.

3) While the pasta is cooking, mix the tomatoes and Pesto and gently warm until they are a little hotter than lukewarm, but not actually cooked (this is easiest to do in a microwave).

4) Two minutes before the pasta is ready (look on the packet for cooking times – they are usually pretty accurate), add the broccoli florets, which will cook during these 2 minutes. As soon as the pasta is done (al dente), drain the pasta and broccoli and mix with the warmed Pesto and tomato. Serve immediately on hot plates.

Spinach and Ricotta Lasagne

Vegetarian lasagne has become a joke dish, like nut cutlets – although in this case usually it is a giveaway sign of tokenism rather than over-the-top worthiness. Where, ten years ago, vegetarians had to survive in public on a diet of leftovers masquerading as omelettes, now there are leftovers masquerading as vegetarian lasagne. I think it is a fairly safe rule that any dish with 'vegetarian' in the title, rather than the actual ingredients (such as spinach and ricotta), has been designed by someone who is more interested in marketing than in what the food actually tastes like. After all, can you imagine what might end up in 'omnivore pie'?

This was the first lasagne we made at The Place Below and, while the recipe has evolved gradually, it is still a favourite. As will be obvious from this and the other recipe in this chapter, I like lasagne with a large proportion of sauce to pasta.

With all lasagne recipes, the final dish is no better than the sauces that make it up, so it is important to season and taste all the constituent bits before putting the lasagne together. In fact, the sauces should lean in the direction of being overseasoned as the pasta has not been cooked in salted water.

SERVES 6–8

FOR THE TOMATO SAUCE

1 medium onion, finely chopped
1 clove of garlic, crushed
50 ml (2 fl oz) olive oil
2 x 400-g (14-oz) tins plum tomatoes, liquidized
1 tsp dried oregano
Salt and freshly ground black pepper

FOR THE SPINACH AND RICOTTA

750 g (1½ lbs) fresh spinach, washed and roughly chopped
450 g (1 lb) ricotta
Salt and freshly ground black pepper
Freshly grated nutmeg, to taste

FOR THE CHEESE SAUCE

50 g (2 oz) butter
50 g (2 oz) plain flour
900 ml (1½ pints) milk

125 g (4 oz) mature cheddar, grated, plus 50 g (2 oz) for sprinkling on top
1 tsp mustard
250 g (9 oz) ready-to-use lasagne

1) Pre-heat the oven to 190°C/375°F/Gas 5.

2) First, make the tomato sauce by sweating the onion and garlic in the olive oil until soft.

3) Add the tomatoes, oregano and seasoning. Bring to the boil and simmer for about 15 minutes. Taste and adjust the seasoning if necessary.

4) For the spinach and ricotta mixture, put the spinach in a large pan over a low to medium heat with the lid on. The remains of the water you washed it in should be enough to start it cooking. Cook for about 5 minutes, then take the pan off the heat. It should be completely wilted and ready to eat.

5) Mix well with the ricotta and season generously with salt and pepper and, more circumspectly, with freshly grated nutmeg. Taste to check the seasoning.

6) Now, make the cheese sauce. Melt the butter and stir in the flour. Cook for 1 minute, stirring constantly. Meanwhile, heat the milk in a separate pan. When the milk is hot, add it, a little at a time, to the flour and butter, stirring vigorously all the time to keep the sauce smooth and shiny. Once all the milk has been added, bring the sauce back to the boil and simmer, still stirring constantly, for 2 to 3 minutes while the sauce thickens.

7) Finally, stir in the cheese and mustard and season to taste with salt and pepper.

8) Assemble the lasagne in the following layers in a deep baking dish measuring about 23 by 33 cm (13 by 9 in):

- small amount of tomato sauce over the bottom of the dish
- lasagne
- tomato sauce
- spinach and ricotta
- lasagne
- tomato sauce
- spinach and ricotta
- lasagne
- cheese sauce
- sprinkling of Cheddar on top.

9) Bake in the pre-heated oven for about 45 minutes, until the pasta is cooked and the top is golden.

Field Mushroom and Aubergine Lasagne

The method for this is exactly the same as for the Spinach and Ricotta Lasagne (see pages 74–5). When constructing the layers, follow step 8, but substitute the mushroom and aubergine sauce for the tomato sauce and the spinach and ricotta mixture.

There are, obviously, endless further variations possible. What I think is necessary for a good lasagne is that one of the constituent parts should provide some acidity (most usually this comes from tomatoes or wine) to contrast with the cheese sauce on top.

SERVES 6–8

FOR THE MUSHROOM AND AUBERGINE SAUCE

750 g (1½ lbs) aubergines, diced
120 ml (4 fl oz) olive oil
Salt and freshly ground black pepper
1 medium onion, finely chopped
1 clove of garlic, crushed
450 g (1 lb) field mushrooms, sliced
1 tsp oregano
1 x 400-g (14-oz) tin plum tomatoes, liquidized

FOR THE CHEESE SAUCE

1 quantity cheese sauce for Spinach and Ricotta Lasagne (see pages 74–5)
250 g (9 oz) ready-to-use lasagne

1) Pre-heat the oven to 220°C/425°F/Gas 7.

2) To make the mushroom and aubergine sauce, toss the aubergines with three quarters of the olive oil and season with salt and pepper. Spread out in a large roasting tin and bake in the pre-heated oven for about 30 minutes, until they are just turning golden and have lost their firmness. Turn the oven down to 190°C/375°F/Gas 5.

3) Meanwhile, sweat the onion and garlic in the remaining olive oil until soft.

4) Add the mushrooms and oregano and cook until the mushrooms are beginning to soften. Add the tomatoes, bring to the boil and simmer for about 15 minutes. Stir in the roast aubergine. Season generously to taste with salt and pepper.

5) Make the cheese sauce as on pages 74–5.

6) Layer the lasagne and sauces in a deep baking dish about 23 by 33 cm (13 by 9 in) as given for the Spinach and Ricotta Lasagne on pages 74–5, step 8, but for tomato and spinach and ricotta sauces read mushroom and aubergine sauce (so, a bit of mushroom, lasagne, mushroom, lasagne, mushroom, lasagne, cheese sauce, sprinkling of cheese). Then, bake in the pre-heated oven for about 45 minutes, until the pasta is cooked and the cheese is bubbling and turning golden.

CHAPTER 6

Bakes and Gratins

Potato, Onion and Gruyère Gratin

Parsnip, Tomato and Gruyère Gratin

Potato, Rosemary and Tomato Bake

Spinach and Ricotta Bake

Courgette and Feta Filo Pie

Mushroom and Ricotta Filo Pie

Lentil, Leek and Parmesan Bake

Potato, Onion and Gruyère Gratin

This and the other two gratin recipes represent the height of real winter comfort food. None of them could be described as slimming, but we do, after all, live in Northern Europe, and there are times when our instincts to build a decent layer of fat to survive a long winter should be followed. In any event, don't substitute single cream for the double, as it will separate. Remember also that these gratins do need a long time in the oven, so do the preparation in plenty of time and then you can forget about it for an hour or more.

We normally serve this gratin with Slow-cooked Red Cabbage and Apple (see page 112), which is somewhat acidic and so cuts through the rich, creamy potato mixture. It is also good with a sharply dressed tomato salad.

SERVES 6

2 medium onions, sliced
2 cloves of garlic, crushed
50 ml (2 fl oz) sunflower oil
150 ml (¼ pint) white wine
450 ml (¾ pint) double cream
1 tsp salt and plenty of freshly ground black pepper
Freshly grated nutmeg, to taste
1.25 kg (2½ lbs) large potatoes, thinly sliced
225 g (8 oz) Gruyère, grated

1) Pre-heat the oven to 190°C/375°F/Gas 5.

2) Sweat the onions and garlic in the sunflower oil until soft.

3) Add the wine, bring to the boil and boil fiercely for a few minutes until the liquid has reduced in volume by half.

4) Add the cream, bring back to the boil, simmer for 1 minute and then take the pan off the heat. Season the sauce with the salt, pepper and a generous grating of nutmeg.

5) Put the potato slices in a large pan of salted water and bring to the boil. Simmer for just under 10 minutes – the potatoes should be not quite cooked. Drain.

6) In a large baking dish, layer the ingredients as follows:

- onion and cream sauce
- potatoes
- onion and cream sauce

- Gruyère
- potatoes
- onion and cream sauce
- potatoes
- onion and cream sauce
- Gruyère.

7) Bake in the pre-heated oven for about 1 hour 15 minutes, until golden brown on top. The potato should have begun to disintegrate into the sauce a bit. You can then serve it immediately or it will quite happily sit in a warm place for an hour or more until you are ready for it.

Parsnip, Tomato and Gruyère Gratin

Frances brought us this recipe, which is adapted from a 1950s cookbook belonging to her mother. The key to its deliciousness is properly seasoning each layer as you construct the gratin.

If the parsnips are sliced very thin the dish can be baked without blanching the parsnips first, but it will take about 2½ hours until the parsnips are tender.

We usually serve this gratin with Savoy cabbage that has been blanched briefly, tossed in a little olive oil and generously seasoned with salt and freshly ground black pepper.

SERVES 6–8

900 g (2 lbs) parsnips, thinly sliced
225 g (8 oz) bread, whizzed into crumbs in a food processor
225 g (8 oz) Gruyère, grated
2 tbsp soft brown sugar
Salt and freshly ground black pepper
1.25 kg (2½ lbs) tomatoes, thinly sliced (preferably plum tomatoes)
600 ml (1 pint) double cream

1) Pre-heat the oven to 190°C/375°F/Gas 5.

2) Bring a large pan of water to the boil. Put the parsnip slices in and bring back to the boil. Boil for 3 minutes, drain and refresh.

3) Mix the breadcrumbs and grated Gruyere together.

4) In a deep baking dish, layer the ingredients, seasoning *each* layer with the sugar and plenty of salt and pepper, to 2.5 cm (1 in) above the top edge of the dish as follows:

   • parsnips
   • tomatoes
   • cheese and breadcrumb mixture
   • parsnips
   • tomatoes
   • cheese and breadcrumb mixture.

5) Pour the cream over the top.

6) Bake in the pre-heated oven for about 1 hour 15 minutes, until the parsnips are completely soft and the tomatoes are disintegrating. Check from time to time.

Potato, Rosemary and Tomato Bake

This is a dish I first made on holiday in a rented cottage, and came about simply because I used up what was in the larder and pinched a bit of rosemary from the landlord's herb garden. Since then, we have cooked it many times at The Place Below.

SERVES 6

750 g (1¾ lbs) large potatoes, finely sliced
225 g (8 oz) mature Cheddar, grated
225 g (8 oz) bread, whizzed into crumbs in a food processor
Salt and freshly ground black pepper
4 finger-length sprigs of rosemary, leaves stripped from the stalks
900 g (2 lbs) tomatoes (preferably plum tomatoes), finely diced
450 ml (¾ pint) double cream

1) Pre-heat the oven to 190°C/375°F/Gas 5.

2) Boil the potatoes for just under 10 minutes, until they are not quite cooked, and drain.

3) Mix the cheese and breadcrumbs together.

4) Layer the ingredients in a deep 23 by 33-cm (9 by 13-in) baking dish, with plenty of salt and freshly ground black pepper on each layer, in the following order:

- potatoes
- rosemary leaves
- tomatoes
- cheese and breadcrumb mixture
- potatoes
- rosemary leaves
- tomatoes
- cheese and breadcrumb mixture.

5) Pour the cream over the top.

6) Bake in the pre-heated oven for about 1 hour 15 minutes, until the top is golden and most of the cream has been absorbed.

Spinach and Ricotta Bake

There are other recipes in this book with spinach and ricotta, but I think this one is my favourite. Served with a Tomato Sauce (see page 126) and some roast New Potatoes with Rosemary (see page 109), it makes a delicious and attractive meal.

SERVES 8

1 medium onion, chopped
2 cloves of garlic, crushed
½ head of celery, finely sliced
2 tbsp sunflower oil
900 g (2 lbs) fresh spinach, washed and roughly chopped
450 g (1 lb) ricotta
2 tbsp single cream
Freshly grated nutmeg, to taste
1 tsp ground coriander
3 eggs
100 g (4 oz) Parmesan, freshly grated
100 g (4 oz) bread, whizzed into crumbs in a food processor

1) Pre-heat the oven to 190°C/375°F/Gas 5.

2) Sweat the onion, garlic and celery in the oil until just cooked.

3) Put the spinach into a large pan over a low heat, covered with a tightly fitting lid. The moisture remaining from washing it should be enough to start it cooking. If not, add a few drops more. As soon as the spinach has completely collapsed (5 minutes or less), take it out of the pan and drain it thoroughly.

4) In a big bowl, combine the ricotta, cream, spices and eggs, mixing thoroughly. Stir in the drained spinach and the onion, garlic and celery. Season well (you may need more seasoning than you expect to offset the blandness of the ricotta).

5) Spoon the mixture into a large (23 by 33-cm/9 by 13-in) greased baking dish. Mix the Parmesan and breadcrumbs together, sprinkle over the top and bake in the pre-heated oven for 35 minutes, until set and golden on top.

Courgette and Feta Filo Pie

Filo pastry has now become a standard ingredient for many home cooks and is readily available in supermarkets and many corner shops. The pastry itself is fat free, being just an extremely thinly rolled layer of a flour and water dough. The seemingly extravagant amount of butter (or oil) you brush between each layer is therefore a necessary part of using it, not a greedy optional extra.

I think that filo is best used in situations where you get a generous amount of filling compared with the amount of pastry. Sometimes individual filo parcels, which can admittedly look very pretty, can suffer from lack of filling. I prefer, therefore, to use it for a family-sized pie, with a generous amount of filling supported and topped by a modest number of layers of pastry.

Filo pastry is easiest to work with when it is thoroughly defrosted but at fridge rather than room temperature (assuming you have bought it frozen, which is how it is usually sold). Once you have taken it out of its wrapper, it dries out quickly and this can make it more difficult to work with. So, unless you work very quickly, it helps to cover the pile of sheets of pastry you haven't got to yet with a slightly damp cloth.

If the sheets of pastry are the wrong size for your baking dish, it is fine to overlap them, cut them or fold them, so long as you always brush melted butter between each layer of pastry.

This recipe was the dish of the day on the day we opened and, although we have refined the method a little, the recipe is still essentially the same, based on an idea from Deborah Madison's excellent *Greens* cookery book (Bantam, 1987).

It makes a big difference to the speed of preparation if you have a grating attachment on your food processor, as there are quite a few courgettes to grate.

We serve this with either a mixed leaf salad or new potatoes boiled and tossed in olive oil. It is also delicious with Patatas bravas à la Place Below (see page 111).

SERVES 6–8

1.5 kg (3 lbs) courgettes, topped, tailed and grated
50 ml (2 fl oz) sunflower oil
100 g (4 oz) Parmesan, freshly grated
175 g (6 oz) feta cheese, crumbled
120 ml (4 fl oz) white wine
1 small onion, very finely chopped
4 eggs
Salt and freshly ground black pepper
50 g (2 oz) butter

1 packet filo pastry, defrosted and chilled
50 g (2 oz) pine nuts

1) Pre-heat the oven to 190°C/375°F/Gas 5.

2) Sweat the grated courgettes in a large pan with the sunflower oil until they are cooked.

3) Turn the cooked courgettes out into a colander to drain off the liquid that will have come out of them (save it for soups or sauces).

4) Return the courgettes to their pan, off the heat, and mix in both the cheeses, the wine, onion and the eggs. Stir well and season generously with salt and pepper.

5) You are now ready to assemble the pie. Make sure you have ready plenty of clean worksurface, a pastry brush and your baking dish (23 by 33 cm/9 by 13 in). Melt the butter in a pan or the microwave. Brush the bottom and sides of the dish with melted butter. Place the first sheet of filo over the bottom of the dish, draping any excess over the sides. Brush the sheet with more melted butter. Repeat with 3 more sheets so that you have 4 sheets altogether for the bottom of the pie. Spread the courgette and feta filling evenly over the filo. Put another layer of filo on top of the filling and brush with melted butter. Repeat with 4 more sheets. Trim any excess pastry with a sharp knife.

6) Scatter the pine nuts on top, then bake in the pre-heated oven for about 35 minutes, until golden brown on top and the filling has set.

Mushroom and Ricotta Filo Pie

225 g (½ lb) leeks, finely sliced
1 clove of garlic, crushed
50 ml (2 fl oz) olive oil
900 g (2 lbs) field mushrooms, sliced
450 g (1 lb) ricotta
100 g (4 oz) Parmesan, freshly grated
2 tbsp soy sauce
3 eggs, beaten
½ bunch of thyme, leaves stripped off the stalks
Salt and freshly ground black pepper
50 g (2 oz) butter, melted
1 packet of filo pastry, defrosted and chilled
½ tsp cumin seeds

1) Pre-heat the oven to 190°C/375°F/Gas 5.

2) Sweat the leeks and garlic in the olive oil until cooked.

3) Add the mushrooms and cook until just soft. Mix in the rest of the ingredients, except the butter, pastry and cumin seeds, and season to taste with salt and pepper.

4) Using the melted butter and filo, make up the pie as described in step 5 for the Courgette and Feta Filo Pie on pages 84–5.

5) Sprinkle the cumin seeds over the top of the pie, then bake in the pre-heated oven for 30 to 40 minutes, until the filling has set and it is turning golden on top.

Lentil, Leek and Parmesan Bake

I would normally run a mile if I saw a lentil bake on a menu, but this is superb (it's even been tested and approved by our local beef cattle farmer). It is based on a dish my sister-in-law, Shirley, dishes up regularly for her family.

It is important to use the ordinary red lentils for this dish, as they are the ones that go mushy best. The quantities may seem vast (it serves ten), but it keeps and reheats excellently and, as it is no more work to make a big one than a little one, why not make life a little easier?

SERVES 10

450 g (1 lb) red lentils
900 ml (1½ pints) water
900 g (2 lbs) leeks, sliced
1 clove of garlic, crushed
50 ml (2 fl oz) olive oil
1 tsp dried tarragon
225 g (8 oz) tomatoes (preferably plum tomatoes), sliced
5 eggs, beaten
275 g (10 oz) Parmesan, freshly grated
Salt and freshly ground black pepper

1) Pre-heat the oven to 200°C/400°F/Gas 6.

2) Put the lentils into a pan with the water. Bring to the boil, then simmer until the lentils are completely soft – you want the consistency of porridge. Add more water during cooking as necessary.

3) In a large pan, sweat the leeks and garlic in the olive oil with the dried tarragon until soft.

4) Take the pan off the heat and mix in the remaining ingredients well. Season to taste.

5) Pour the mixture into a deep 33 by 23-cm (13 by 9-in) baking dish and bake in the pre-heated oven for about 45 minutes, until it has set and is beginning to turn golden on top.

CHAPTER 7

Salads and Cold Main Dishes

Roquefort Terrine

Cashew and Mushroom Terrine

Aubergine Salad with Pine Nuts, Raisins and Balsamic Vinegar

Roast Mediterranean Vegetables with Tomato Vinaigrette and Grilled Halloumi

Wild Rice and Sun-dried Tomato Salad

Puy Lentils with Roast Fennel

Tabbouleh

Bart's Bulgar Wheat Salad

Mushrooms and Fine Beans à la Grecque

Marinated Oriental Vegetables

Pasta Salad with Teriyaki Cashews, Almonds and Pistachios

Broccoli and Carrots with Mint and Parsley

Roquefort Terrine

I think this is one of the most delicious, as well as one of the simplest, dishes we make at The Place Below.

Sarah and I often stay near Cordes, a beautiful mediaeval town near Toulouse. We have once been to the local (extremely grand) Michelin-starred establishment called Le Grand Écuyer. We went with a group of friends and, between us, presented a fairly challenging set of dietary requirements: two vegetarians, one vegetarian who eats fish, a Jew wishing to be as kosher as possible, one who wished to eat only puddings (there was something called a 'menu douceur', which included four pudding courses) and Sarah, who will eat whatever is put on her plate, except rice pudding. The restaurant responded superbly, offering a vegetarian menu I have never seen remotely paralleled in France, and which starred a Roquefort terrine.

Since then, our version of this dish has become a standard at The Place Below. It is best served with something sweet, such as really ripe Canteloupe melon, poached pears or roast sweet potato, and some baby spinach leaves, seasoned and dressed with walnut oil.

This is an extremely rich terrine, so do not make the portions too large. For a starter-sized piece, cut the terrine into about eight slices, then cut each slice diagonally in two, giving one bit to each person. For a main course, serve a whole slice per person.

SERVES 8

100 g (4 oz) Lexia raisins (the plumpest and best, available from healthfood shops)
50 ml (2 fl oz) brandy
450 g (1 lb) Roquefort
350 g (12 oz) cream cheese
100 g (4 oz) walnut pieces

1) Soak the raisins in the brandy overnight.

2) The next day, crumble the Roquefort into a big bowl. Using your hands, mix in all the other ingredients gently.

3) Line a 900-g (2-lb) loaf tin with cling film. Press the Roquefort mixture down into the lined tin. Wrap the surplus clingfilm over the top and weigh down well for several hours or overnight.

4) Turn the terrine out and slice – I find this easiest with a serrated knife, using a sawing motion – into 8.

Cashew and Mushroom Terrine

All food has a history. This terrine is another dish that Ian used to make at Bart's.

These quantities are for a 900-g (2-lb) loaf tin, which will serve around ten portions and is meant to be served cold. However, it's a highly flexible dish that is also delicious hot. It'll also be even better if you can cook it the night before you need it.

Serve it with Onion Marmalade (see page 122) and Broccoli and Carrots with Mint and Parsley (see page 103).

SERVES 10

1 large onion, finely chopped
50 ml (2 fl oz) sunflower oil
350 g (12 oz) field mushrooms, finely chopped
100 g (4 oz) fresh tomatoes (preferably plum tomato), skinned and finely chopped
25 g (1 oz) plain flour
2 tsp Marmite
40 ml (1½ fl oz) red wine, diluted with the same quantity of water
1 tbsp chopped fresh parsley
225 g (8 oz) cashews, a handful left whole, the rest ground in a blender or food processor
100 g (4 oz) breadcrumbs, preferably from stale wholemeal bread
2 tbsp tahini
Salt and freshly ground black pepper

1) Pre-heat the oven to 220°C/425°F/Gas 7.

2) Fry the onion in the sunflower oil until soft.

3) Add the mushrooms and cook for 5 minutes.

4) Add the tomatoes and cook for 2 more minutes.

5) Stir in the flour and cook for 1 minute, stirring continuously. Add the Marmite and diluted wine and cook until thick.

6) Mix in the parsley, ground cashews, breadcrumbs and tahini and season to taste with a little salt and lots of pepper.

7) Oil a 900-g (2-lb) loaf tin and line with greaseproof paper. Pack the mushroom and nut mixture into the tin and cover with greaseproof paper and foil.

8) Bake in the pre-heated oven for about 50 minutes until firm. Leave to cool, then refrigerate. When ready to serve, slice carefully with a serrated knife into 10.

Aubergine Salad with Pine Nuts, Raisins and Balsamic Vinegar

I came to aubergines late in life, but I am now making up for lost time. Until recently, I would never have thought of them as a salad ingredient; now I think that they are one of the best and most luxurious. There are only two methods we use for cooking aubergine: roasting or baking whole. (If we had a grill there would be a third method, but producing 150 lunches each day from a kitchen the same size as a bedsit I once had, we have to be disciplined in our choice of kitchen equipment!)

There are two keys to delicious roast aubergine. First, cook them with plenty of olive oil and salt, and, second, cook them for long enough – the flesh should be collapsed and soft, not chewy.

This delicious dish was one Frances made soon after she arrived at The Place Below. The sweet and sour combination of balsamic vinegar and plump raisins works with the rich roast aubergine. Delicious on bruschetta (toast brushed with olive oil and garlic) for a starter, or with Tabbouleh (see page 97) and Haricot Bean and Roast Garlic Purée (see page 115).

SERVES 6

900 g (2 lbs) aubergine, cubed
150 ml (¼ pint) olive oil
Salt and freshly ground black pepper
1 tbsp balsamic vinegar
50 g (2 oz) pine nuts, toasted
50 g (2 oz) raisins, preferably Lexia
1 bunch of flat-leaf parsley, roughly chopped

1) Pre-heat the oven to 220°C/425°F/Gas 7.

2) Put the aubergine cubes into a large bowl and toss thoroughly with the olive oil. Season generously with salt and pepper. Spread them out over a couple of baking sheets – if you have bits of aubergine on top of one another, ones that are covered up will not roast properly. Bake the aubergine in the pre-heated oven for about 30 minutes, until the white flesh is turning golden and there is not much resistance when you prod.

3) In a large bowl, gently mix the roasted aubergine with the remaining ingredients. Check the seasoning. You can serve this salad either warm or at room temperature.

Roast Mediterranean Vegetables with
Tomato Vinaigrette and Grilled Halloumi

The flavours of this dish are those of a piquant version of ratatouille, with the tomato vinaigrette replacing the tomato sauce of the ratatouille. This would be great for a summer dinner party, served with Fresh Herb Olive Oil Bread made with basil (see page 18).

The halloumi can be either grilled or fried in a little olive oil.

SERVES 6

2 large aubergines, cubed
120 ml (4 fl oz) olive oil, plus extra if necessary
Salt and freshly ground black pepper
450 g (1 lb) courgettes, sliced fairly chunkily
2 red peppers, deseeded and chopped in 8 lengthways
2 yellow peppers, deseeded and chopped in 8 lengthways
Small bunch of basil, finely chopped
375 g (12 oz) halloumi cheese, cut into strips

FOR THE DRESSING

1 ripe plum tomato, peeled and roughly chopped
1 tbsp white wine vinegar
1 tbsp water
1 clove of garlic, crushed
90 ml (3 fl oz) olive oil

1) Pre-heat the oven to 220°C/425°F/Gas 7.

2) Place the aubergine cubes in a large mixing bowl, toss with half the olive oil and season well with salt and pepper. Spread the aubergine cubes out on one or two large baking sheets so they are separate and bake in the pre-heated oven for about 30 minutes, until the flesh is very soft (a partially raw aubergine is not a pleasant thing) but the skins not at all burnt. Remove from the oven and set aside.

3) Repeat the process with the courgettes and the peppers. The courgettes will take no more than 15 minutes (if the oven is up to temperature) and should still have some texture. The peppers take about 20 minutes, until they are just colouring and losing their firmness.

4) Place all the roast vegetables, together with the basil and any cooking juices left on the baking sheets, back in a large mixing bowl.

5) To make the dressing, place the tomato, vinegar and water in a small saucepan. Bring to the boil, cover and simmer gently for 15 minutes. Strain the mixture through a sieve, add the garlic, then slowly whisk in the olive oil. The mixture should emulsify to make a thick sauce. Season to taste.

6) Pour the dressing over the vegetables and basil, turn gently to coat them and place in a serving dish. Do not refrigerate as, like most salads, this dish tastes much better at room temperature than straight out of the fridge.

7) Just before you are ready to serve, pre-heat the grill. Place the strips of halloumi on a lightly oiled baking sheet and grill for 2 to 3 minutes until hot. Arrange the halloumi on the salad and serve immediately with thick slices of fresh, crusty bread or a bulgar wheat or rice salad – something to mop up the lovely juices!

Wild Rice and Sun-dried Tomato Salad

Wild rice is notoriously expensive, but it is delicious. So as not to be completely bankrupted, don't buy it in very small quantities and buy it at healthfood shops, not supermarkets. Don't bother with the mixes of wild and other rices – you will be paying significantly more than the price of good-quality basmati, while getting little or none of the flavour of wild rice. Similarly, I don't think there's much to recommend recipes that suggest mixing wild rice with other grains.

Despite the fact that, technically, it is not a member of the rice family, wild rice cooks in a very similar way to unprocessed, wholegrain rice. It normally takes about 40 minutes, but if you cook it in a stock like risotto, it can take more than twice that time.

Wild rice is a superb basis for salads, both because of its unique earthy aroma and taste, and because it is fairly robust and does not collapse into a sticky mess when stirred together with other ingredients. As with Puy lentils, it goes particularly well with powerful flavours, such as this combination of a fresh tomato vinaigrette with sun-dried tomatoes.

Some consumers' disillusion with sun-dried tomatoes stems from using them as they are without soaking. They must be soaked for about 30 minutes in hot water if you buy them dried (as opposed to preserved in oil). If you wish to preserve your own in oil, be sure to drain them extremely thoroughly after soaking and before putting them in the olive oil or they will go mouldy.

SERVES 6

1.2 litres (2 pints) water
1 tsp salt
225 g (8 oz) wild rice
25 g (1 oz) dried sun-dried tomatoes or 50 g (2 oz) if they are preserved in oil
½ bunch of coriander, leaves picked from the stalks
2 tbsp soy sauce

FOR THE TOMATO VINAIGRETTE

1 clove of garlic, crushed
1 smallish fresh tomato (preferably a plum tomato)
2 tbsp balsamic vinegar
120 ml (4 fl oz) olive oil

1) Put the water into a pan with the salt. Bring to the boil. Pour the wild rice in, bring back to the boil, then simmer, covered, for about 40 minutes, until the grains are tender and beginning to split open to reveal a paler interior.

2) While the rice is cooking prepare the sun-dried tomatoes. If you have the kind preserved in oil, simply take them from the jar and chop them finely. If you buy them in their dried state (and they are cheaper this way), then put them in a bowl, pour boiling water over them and leave them to soak for 30 minutes. Then drain them and chop them finely.

3) Next, make the tomato vinaigrette. Put the garlic, tomato and vinegar into a blender and whizz until smooth. While still blending, pour in the olive oil gradually. The dressing should emulsify like a mayonnaise.

4) Mix the cooked rice, vinaigrette, sun-dried tomatoes, coriander and soy sauce together. Check the seasoning, then serve either warm or at room temperature.

Puy Lentils with Roast Fennel

I think it's a mistake to try to make every dish look like an artist's palette. Some ingredients do not lend them themselves to the 'rainbow' style of food presentation. Puy lentils (small slate-green lentils from the area around the French town of Le Puy) fall into this category, so don't abuse them by sticking in bits of sweetcorn or diced pepper in a vain attempt to 'brighten them up'.

Don't substitute red lentils in a salad like this as they will disintegrate into a mush. The larger brown or green lentils could be used, but I don't think they taste so nice.

Puy lentils are one of the most delicious and adaptable pulses and go particularly well with strong flavours such as balsamic vinegar and fennel or hefty dressings featuring chillies and sun-dried tomatoes.

Serve this dish as part of a summer plate, perhaps with Tabbouleh (see page 97) and a green salad or Roast Mediterranean Vegetables with Tomato and Vinaigrette and Grilled Halloumi (see pages 92–3).

SERVES 6 AS PART OF A SALAD PLATE

175 g (6 oz) Puy lentils
2 fennel bulbs, sliced
250 ml (8 fl oz) olive oil
50 ml (2 fl oz) balsamic vinegar
2 tbsp soy sauce
Freshly ground black pepper
1 bunch of flat-leaf parsley, chopped, to garnish

1) Put the lentils into a pan with plenty of water and bring to the boil. Simmer for 35 minutes, until just tender. Drain.

2) Sweat the fennel in one third of the olive oil until tender.

3) While the lentils are still warm, stir in the vinegar and soy sauce. Then stir in the fennel and remaining olive oil. Season well with pepper. Garnish with the parsley and serve at room temperature or warmer – never straight from the fridge.

Tabbouleh

This is a salad you see everywhere now. It has endless variants (on both the ingredients and the spelling), but is at its best when it is kept simple and fresh. This is Ian's version and the key elements are to use plenty of fresh lemon juice, parsley and mint. As to curly versus flat-leaf parsley, I prefer the flat-leaf type, but either is acceptable here.

We serve Tabbouleh with Hummus (see page 114) and some roast vegetables – maybe red onions and peppers. In summer, it's hard for us to make enough of it. We also serve it warm with Ratatouille (see pages 40–41) and Hummus.

SERVES 6 AS PART OF A SELECTION

450 ml (¾ pint) water
225 g (8 oz) bulgar wheat
Salt

FOR THE DRESSING

1 clove of garlic, crushed
Juice of 1 large lemon
85 ml (3 fl oz) olive oil
1 bunch of parsley, leaves picked from the stalks and finely chopped
1 bunch of mint, leaves picked from the stalks and finely chopped

1) Put the water into a large pan and bring to the boil. Add the bulgar wheat and some salt. If it is fine bulgar wheat (this looks like a slightly darker version of couscous), turn off the heat straightaway and leave it, covered, to soak up the water for about 10 minutes. If it is coarse bulgar wheat (which looks rather like demerara sugar), bring back to the boil and simmer, stirring occasionally for about 5 minutes, until all the water is absorbed. Set aside and allow to cool. (If you don't allow the bulgar wheat to cool, you will cook the fresh herbs, which is not the idea.)

2) Mix all the other ingredients together, pour over the cooled bulgar wheat and mix thoroughly. Check the seasoning and serve. Although it is at its best when freshly made, it will keep quite happily for a couple of days in the fridge in a sealed container. As with any salads stored in the fridge, allow it to come to room temperature before serving.

Bart's Bulgar Wheat Salad

In Ian's previous restaurant, Bart's (named after a particularly soppy dog), they always served a trio of salads. When I ate there, both as cook standing in for Ian when he went on holiday and customer, I never tired of this simple salad.

It looks a somewhat murky brown colour, but is delicious as part of a summer table of salads. It keeps well for a couple of days. If you are not used to cooking with bulgar wheat, see the note on the different available types and how to cook them on page 97.

SERVES 6 AS PART OF A SALAD PLATE

FOR THE SALAD

225 g (8 oz) bulgar wheat
600 ml (1 pint) boiling water
100 g (4 oz) raisins
100 g (4 oz) sunflower seeds

FOR THE DRESSING

2 tsp Dijon mustard
4 tbsp soy sauce
1½ tbsp white wine vinegar
175 ml (6 fl oz) olive oil

1) Soak the bulgar wheat in the boiling water until all the water has been absorbed. If you are using coarse bulgar wheat, you will need to simmer it until the water has been absorbed.

2) Make the dressing by mixing all the dressing ingredients together.

3) Pour the dressing over the soaked bulgar wheat. Add the raisins and sunflower seeds and mix well.

Mushrooms and Fine Beans à la Grecque

Sarah and I spent three months in Cornwall testing all these recipes with domestic quantities and equipment. We stayed in a marvellous converted barn on the Helford River belonging to Charlie and Barbara Pugh. Despite farming beef cattle, they were extremely enthusiastic recipients of our leftovers — in fact, there were plenty of mutterings about being very happy living on a vegetarian diet. This salad in particular went down a storm, and they tell me it's also excellent served hot.

If you prefer a slightly spicier version of this, mix the harissa into the reduced sauce before marinating the vegetables.

SERVES 6 AS PART OF A SALAD PLATE

2 cloves of garlic, crushed
1 medium onion, finely chopped
2 tbsp olive oil
450 g (1 lb) button mushrooms or small chestnut mushrooms, halved
1 tbsp coriander seeds, toasted and ground
2 bay leaves
175 g (6 oz) fresh tomatoes (preferably plum tomatoes), skinned and chopped
300 ml (½ pint) red wine
1 tsp molasses sugar or other dark brown sugar
1 tbsp soy sauce
275 g (10 oz) fine green beans, topped, tailed and halved
½ bunch of flat-leaf parsley, roughly chopped, to garnish
¼ tsp Harissa (see page 119 — optional)

1) Cook the garlic and onion in the olive oil until soft.

2) Add the mushrooms, coriander seeds and bay leaves and sweat until the mushrooms are just going soft.

3) Add the tomatoes, wine, sugar, soy sauce and beans. Simmer, covered, until the beans are just done.

4) Drain in a colander set over a large bowl and put the vegetables on one side. Return the sauce to the pan and bring to the boil. Boil fiercely, uncovered, until the sauce has reduced in volume by half. Add the Harissa, if using.

5) Pour the sauce over the vegetables and leave to marinate for a couple of hours, turning occasionally. Garnish with the parsley and serve at room temperature.

Marinated Oriental Vegetables

This is an aromatic and highly textured salad that Frances makes regularly at The Place Below. If you are serving it as a main course, you might add soy-roasted cashews. Blanched asparagus and briefly sautéed shiitake mushrooms are also delicious additions if you're feeling extravagant.

How long you blanch the vegetables for is, to some extent, a matter of taste, but, for a dish such as this, they should retain a good deal of crunch. The easiest way to blanch a succession of vegetables, each of which may take a slightly different amount of time, is as follows. Have a good-sized pan of water boiling, then put each vegetable in turn into a chip basket and dunk it into the water for the required length of time. The vegetables can then be easily drained, turned out into a waiting basin of cold water to stop them cooking further and then drained in a colander as soon as they have cooled down.

SERVES 6

100 g (4 oz) sugar-snap peas, topped and tailed
100 g (4 oz) baby corn, sliced in half lengthways
100 g (4 oz) carrots, sliced diagonally
100 g (4 oz) broccoli, divided into small florets
1 red pepper, deseeded and cut into strips
4 spring onions, finely chopped
100 g (4 oz) beansprouts

FOR THE DRESSING

1 clove of garlic
1-cm (½-in) slice fresh root ginger, peeled
2 tbsp balsamic or red wine vinegar
2 tbsp soy sauce
2½ tbsp sesame oil
2½ tbsp sunflower oil
1 bunch of coriander, washed and roughly chopped

1) Blanch the sugar-snaps for 1 minute, the baby corn for 2 minutes, the carrots for 2 minutes and the broccoli for 1 minute, then refresh them in cold water as described in the introduction to this recipe. Drain thoroughly.

2) Make the dressing. Place the garlic and ginger in a food processor with the balsamic or red wine vinegar and soy sauce. Whizz until smooth then, while still whizzing, gradually add both kinds of oil.

3) Put all the vegetables, except the beansprouts, together with the dressing and coriander, into a large, flat dish. Turn the vegetables gently to coat them with the dressing and leave at room temperature for 1 to 2 hours, remembering to turn a few times during this period. (This salad is best made on the day it is to be eaten as the dressing will eventually discolour the vegetables.) Add the beansprouts just before serving.

Pasta Salad with Teriyaki Cashews, Almonds and Pistachios

This is not one of those anaemic and soggy-looking pasta salads you see languishing in plastic tubs in second-rate delicatessens. This is a great mixture of powerful flavours and contrasting textures.

The nuts are cooked in something approaching a teriyaki sauce (please, no letters telling me that this is not how you make an *authentic* teriyaki sauce – ours tastes delicious and that's the point) and they make a delicious snack on their own. They also combine beautifully with the pasta and raisins. We often serve this salad with some mixed leaves and Broccoli and Carrots with Mint and Parsley (see page 103).

SERVES 4–6 AS PART OF A SALAD PLATE

50 g (2 oz) cashew nuts
50 g (2 oz) pistachios
50 g (2 oz) almonds
50 ml (2 fl oz) soy sauce
85 ml (3 fl oz) red wine
2 tbsp molasses sugar
120 ml (4 fl oz) olive oil
225 g (8 oz) dried pasta, such as penne or fusilli
2 tbsp balsamic vinegar
100 g (4 oz) raisins, preferably Lexia

1) Put the nuts into a frying pan with the soy sauce, wine, sugar and one quarter of the olive oil. Boil fiercely, stirring continuously, coating and recoating the nuts until the liquid has almost evaporated and the nuts are covered in a thick goo. Take the pan off the heat and set on one side.

2) Cook the pasta in plenty of water until just cooked. Drain it and toss with the rest of the olive oil and the vinegar. Mix in the nuts and raisins and serve warm or at room temperature.

Broccoli and Carrots with Mint and Parsley

I am always excited to find we have introduced a customer to an ingredient they thought they hated. This simple and delicious salad has converted at least one established broccoli hater. It looks and tastes great and can be served hot or at room temperature, but is definitely a dish that needs to be eaten soon after it's made – old, refrigerated, cooked broccoli is no fun.

SERVES 4–6 AS AN ACCOMPANIMENT

375 g (12 oz) carrots
375 g (12 oz) broccoli
50 ml (2 fl oz) olive oil
½ bunch of mint, *leaves picked from the stalks and chopped*
½ bunch of parsley (*preferably flat-leaf variety*), *leaves picked from the stalks and chopped*
Salt and freshly ground black pepper

1) Peel the carrots and slice them fairly thickly diagonally. (If the carrots are very large, cut them in half lengthways first.)

2) Divide the broccoli into florets. Take the woody bits off the stalks and then slice the stalks finely.

3) Bring a large pan of salted water to the boil. Boil the carrots for 2 minutes, then add the broccoli and boil for 2 more minutes.

4) If you are going to serve the vegetables hot, drain them thoroughly – broccoli can hold a lot of water. Then, toss them in the oil and herbs while still warm, season, taste to check the seasoning and serve.

5) If you are going to serve the vegetables at room temperature, refresh them in cold water as soon as you take them out of the boiling water to prevent them cooking further, then drain thoroughly. Toss them in the oil and herbs just before serving. Do not forget to season and taste.

CHAPTER 8

Hot Accompaniments and Side Vegetables

Special Mashed Potatoes
Smoked Cheddar
Pesto
Tahini

Swede, Carrot and Potato Purée

Celeriac and Potato Mash

Hot Roast Vegetables
Chilli and Garlic Roast Potato Wedges
Sage Roast Butternut Squash
New Potatoes with Rosemary
Roast Sweet Potatoes

Patatas Bravas à la Place Below

Slow-cooked Red Cabbage and Apple

Special Mashed Potatoes

I love mashed potatoes – both ordinary buttery, peppery mashed potatoes and more exotic versions, flavoured with herbs or spicy sauces. Here are some combinations we have found work particularly well, but don't be afraid to experiment. Just be sure that the flavour of the mashed potato goes well with whatever you are serving with it.

All the flavourings below are to be added to 900 g (2 lbs) tender potatoes. At home, I often don't peel potatoes for making mash ('Sacrilege', I hear the chefs' union cry), although in the restaurant we pander to our customers' prejudices and use peeled potatoes for this purpose. So, do whatever you prefer – at home you only have to please yourselves and your friends.

To avoid the mash going glutinous, it is important to do the mashing when the potatoes are still hot and before you add anything to them. If you are making a traditional mash with butter and milk, it also helps to heat the butter and milk before adding them. Whatever kind you are making, don't forget to keep tasting – let your tastebuds guide you as to how much seasoning to add.

SERVES 4–6

Smoked Cheddar Mashed Potatoes

This is delicious with Guinness and Mushroom Casserole (see pages 38–9).

150 ml (¼ pint) milk, warmed
50 g (2 oz) butter, warmed with the milk
100 g (4 oz) smoked Cheddar, grated

Pesto Mashed Potatoes

We serve this with Place Below Ratatouille (see pages 40–41). It is good with any casserole with a tomato-based sauce, and makes a marvellous snack accompanied by a tomato salad. The quantity of Pesto specified makes for a fairly strong-tasting mash – some people may prefer a little less.

175 g (6 oz) Pesto (see pages 117–18)

Tahini Mashed Potatoes

175 g (6 oz) Spicy Tahini Sauce (see page 116)
50 ml (2 fl oz) olive oil

Swede, Carrot and Potato Purée

Swede has a reputation as bad as that acquired by prunes, but, to my mind, it is equally undeserved — just because they were ingredients with which school cooks used to do appalling things, doesn't mean we can't redeem them as adults. Mashed with potato, puréed carrot and either butter or olive oil, it makes a delicious and pretty accompaniment. Try it with Field Mushroom, Puy Lentil and Fresh Thyme Casserole (see pages 51–2).

SERVES 6

350 g (12 oz) carrots, thickly sliced
450 g (1 lb) swede, peeled and cubed
350 g (12 oz) potatoes, cubed
75 g (3 oz) butter and 85 ml (3 fl oz) milk or 120 ml (4 fl oz) olive oil
Salt and freshly ground black pepper

1) Put all the vegetables into a large pan with a lot of water. Bring to the boil, then simmer until the potatoes are done (they will take longest).

2) Drain thoroughly and mash well with a potato masher.

3) Meanwhile, warm the milk and butter, if using, in a pan until nearly boiling. Pour the hot milk and butter or the oil over the vegetables and stir quickly (if using the butter and milk, heating them helps to stop the vegetables becoming glutinous). Season well to taste with salt and pepper.

Celeriac and Potato Mash

For me, this is the prince of all mash. I love the creamy texture and celery-like aroma of celeriac. Serve this with Pepperonata and Stilton (see page 54) or any of the mushroom-based casseroles.

SERVES 4–6

450 g (1 lb) celeriac, peeled and diced
450 g (1 lb) potatoes, peeled and diced
150 ml (¼ pint) milk, warmed
50 g (2 oz) butter, warmed with the milk
Salt and freshly ground black pepper

1) Boil the celeriac and potatoes in separate pans until each is tender, then drain.

2) Put the cooked celeriac into a food processor with the warmed milk and butter and whizz until smooth.

3) Mash the potato with a potato masher, then mix in the celeriac purée. Don't whizz the potato in the blender, as it will go glutinous. Season to taste with salt and pepper.

Hot Roast Vegetables

Roast winter vegetables are one of the things we do well in Northern Europe, and similar methods can be used with newer arrivals such as butternut squash and sweet potatoes. Like mashed potatoes, roast parsnips and spicy roast potatoes are things designed to make people happy, not make them boggle at the skill and originality of the cook.

The only technical matter to be aware of is that some root vegetables (notably maincrop potatoes and parsnips) benefit greatly from parboiling (being boiled until almost cooked) before roasting, whereas for other vegetables this is unnecessary. Also, a lot of cookbooks suggest that roasting vegetables should sit in the oven in a bath of hot fat, but I prefer the result when they are coated in a relatively thin layer of fat. This also means you don't find yourself edging around the kitchen nervously carrying a dish of boiling oil.

Chilli and Garlic Roast Potato Wedges

I really think these are much better made with *unpeeled* potatoes. The roast potato skin is quite as delicious as the main bit of the potato.

SERVES 6

---

900 g (2 lbs) large potatoes
50 ml (2 fl oz) sunflower oil
½ fresh chilli, finely chopped with seeds
2 cloves of garlic, crushed
Salt

1) Pre-heat the oven to 220°C/425°F/Gas 7.

2) Cut the potatoes into wedges and boil until just cooked.

3) Toss them in the oil, spices and add plenty of salt. Put them in a roasting tin and bake in the pre-heated oven for about 30 minutes (it may take considerably longer, though, if the oven is full of other things), until crisp on the outside. Lift them from the roasting tin with a slotted spoon, leaving any excess oil behind.

Sage Roast Butternut Squash

If you have not discovered butternut squash, it is a simple and delicious vegetable to try, now widely available in supermarkets.

SERVES 4

675 g (1½ lbs) butternut squash
50 ml (2 fl oz) olive oil
20 fresh sage leaves, finely chopped
Salt and freshly ground black pepper

1) Pre-heat the oven to 220°C/425°F/Gas 7.

2) Cut the squash in half lengthways and deseed and peel it. Cut it into long wedges, about 15 in all. (It is not essential to peel it, but the skin can be a little tough after roasting.)

3) In a large roasting tin, toss the squash wedges with the oil and sage and season well with salt and pepper, then bake in the pre-heated oven for 30 to 40 minutes, until the squash feels tender when you insert a sharp knife.

New Potatoes with Rosemary

These are incredibly simple to do, and delicious. Serve them with any of the quiches or tarts in Chapter 4. They are also brilliant as a pre-dinner nibble, served with Spicy Tahini Sauce (page 116) as a dip.

SERVES 4–6

900 g (2 lbs) new potatoes
50 ml (2 fl oz) olive oil
2 tsp dried rosemary
Salt and freshly ground black pepper

1) Pre-heat the oven to 220°C/425°F/Gas 7.

2) Toss the potatoes in the oil and rosemary and season well with salt and pepper, then bake in the pre-heated oven for about 40 to 50 minutes, until tender (test them with a sharp knife or by eating one).

Roast Sweet Potatoes

Roast Sweet Potatoes are delicious eaten hot with Chilli Bean Casserole (page 44) or Boston Beans (see page 48), as well as being a great salad ingredient.

Use the orange-fleshed variety. The more common white-fleshed variety is acceptable served hot, but still inferior. It is not always easy to tell one from the other by the skin colour if you are not familiar with the vegetable, but the pinker skin indicates white flesh and the browner skin indicates orange flesh.

SERVES 4

750 g (1½ lbs) medium, orange-fleshed sweet potatoes
50 ml (2 fl oz) sunflower oil
Salt and freshly ground black pepper

1) Pre-heat the oven to 220°C/425°F/Gas 7.

2) Cut each sweet potato into wedges; there's no need to peel them. Toss them in the sunflower oil and salt and pepper, then spread them out on a large baking sheet and roast in the pre-heated oven for about 30 minutes, until a thin knife goes in smoothly and without much pressure needing to be applied.

Patatas bravas à la Place Below

I have never been to Spain (more's the pity) and I have never eaten patatas bravas except at The Place Below, so this may not be an authentic recipe. It is, however, delicious and is my interpretation of what Frances told me they should be like. It combines brilliantly with the Courgette and Feta Filo Pie (see pages 84–5), but I could also quite happily eat a plateful of it on its own.

(see pages 84–5)

SERVES 6

900 g (2 lbs) new potatoes
120 ml (4 fl oz) olive oil
Salt and freshly ground black pepper
1 onion, halved and finely sliced
2 cloves of garlic, crushed
½ fresh red chilli, finely chopped with seeds
1 x 400-g (14-oz) tin plum tomatoes, liquidized

1) Pre-heat the oven to 220°C/425°F/Gas 7.

2) Cut the new potatoes in half lengthways. Toss in half the olive oil and some salt and pepper. Spread them out in a roasting tin and bake in the pre-heated oven for about 30 minutes, until they are becoming crisp on the outside and are cooked in the middle.

3) Meanwhile, make the tomato sauce. Sweat the onion, garlic and chilli in the rest of the olive oil until soft.

4) Add the tomatoes, bring to the boil, then simmer for about 10 to 15 minutes. Stir in the roast potatoes and season to taste. This can be served at once or reheated.

Slow-cooked Red Cabbage and Apple

I have experimented a lot with different red cabbage and apple recipes and this, for me, is the definitive version. It does need to cook for a long time, so don't make it unless you can be near the kitchen for a couple of hours to keep an eye on it. It goes particularly well with rich and creamy dishes such as the Potato, Onion and Gruyère Gratin (see pages 79–80).

Note that it does not require salt.

SERVES 4

450 g (1 lb) red cabbage, cored and finely sliced
50 ml (2 fl oz) sunflower oil
180 ml (6 fl oz) red wine
2 eating apples, peeled and finely diced
2 tbsp molasses sugar
2 tbsp white wine vinegar
2 tbsp redcurrant jelly

1) Sweat the cabbage in the oil for about 10 minutes.

2) Add the wine, turn up the heat and cook until the liquid has reduced by half.

3) Add the rest of the ingredients, cover and simmer over the lowest possible heat for 2 hours. After that time, turn up the heat, take off the lid and boil fiercely until the liquid has reduced to a sticky goo at the bottom of the pan. Serve.

CHAPTER 9

Pâtés, Relishes, Dressings and Sauces

Hummus

Haricot Bean and Roast Garlic Purée

Spicy Tahini Sauce

Pesto

Harissa

Guacamole

Cucumber, Apple and Mint Relish

Onion Marmalade

Vinaigrette

Honey and Ginger Dressing

Rich Dill Dressing

Tomato Sauce

Roast Marinated Tofu

Hummus

For me, 'simplest is best' with hummus. What makes the difference between good hummus and boring hummus, however, is plenty of fresh lemon juice and decent olive oil. Extras like cumin or coriander miss the point, which is that it should have a velvety texture and a simple but well-balanced flavour.

For those who are interested in such things, hummus, like beans on toast, provides a good balance of amino acids (the building blocks of protein) with its combination of pulses (chickpeas) and seeds (tahini is made from crushed sesame seeds), while being free of dairy products. In my optimistic view of the world, things that taste good, year in, year out, are often later discovered to have a nutritionally balanced or beneficial make-up. The combination of rice and dal is a similar example – grains provide most of the amino acids lacking in pulses. It was, therefore, no surprise to me to be told that drinking wine in moderation is also good for you.

MAKES ABOUT 450 G (1 LB)

225 g (8 oz) dried chickpeas
50 g (2 oz) pale tahini
Juice of 2 lemons
1 clove of garlic
150 ml (¼ pint) chickpea cooking liquid
85 ml (3 fl oz) olive oil
Salt and freshly ground black pepper

1) Soak the chickpeas overnight in heavily salted water.

2) The next day, drain the chickpeas from their soaking water and put in a pan with 1.2 litres (2 pints) of fresh water. Bring to the boil, boil fiercely for 10 minutes, then cover and simmer for about 1 hour, until the chickpeas are very tender. Drain but retain all the cooking liquid (what you don't use in this recipe is good for making soup).

3) Put the chickpeas into a blender and purée with all the other ingredients, except the oil and seasoning, and whizz until you have a smooth paste. While still whizzing, pour in the olive oil. Season to taste with salt and pepper.

Haricot Bean and Roast Garlic Purée

Hummus is one of the extraordinary ingredients of the transformation that has taken place in British eating habits. Twenty years ago, only wholefood fanatics and anthropologists had even heard of it, but now it is a totally standard part of many a summer buffet. But, if chickpeas and sesame paste are nice puréed together, what about other pulses with other flavours? Is this garlic and haricot bean purée a new classic of the future? Will there be taste tests to compare 20 different supermarket versions?

Such fanciful imagining aside, I think it is delicious and richly flavoured. We serve a blob of it on our ratatouille and just like hummus, with roasted vegetables and tabbouleh. You could also use it as a dip with crudités.

MAKES ABOUT 450 G (1 LB) OF PURÉE

225 g (8 oz) dried haricot beans
100 g (4 oz) garlic
Juice of 2 lemons
2 or 3 juniper berries, lightly crushed
3 tbsp water
1 tsp salt
50 ml (2 fl oz) olive oil

1) Soak the haricot beans overnight.

2) Next day, pre-heat the oven to 220°C/425°F/Gas 7.

3) Drain the beans and boil them in plenty of fresh water for about 1 hour, until very tender.

4) Break the garlic into cloves, but do not peel them. Spread them out on a baking sheet and bake in the pre-heated oven for about 10 minutes, until just tender. (If you have not cooked garlic in this way before, look at the method on page 25). Leave to cool, then peel the cloves of garlic.

5) Blend the garlic, lemon juice, juniper berries and water with half the salt in a food processor. Add the beans and continue blending. Slowly add the oil. Check the seasoning and add a bit more water if necessary to achieve the desired consistency.

Spicy Tahini Sauce

In the weeks before and just after opening the restaurant, I was saved from madness by a wise American chef called Pam Knutsen. Since she has gone back to live in Minneapolis, we have regularly exchanged thoughts and recipes. This sauce is based on one served at Café Brenda in Minneapolis, where Pam has often worked since going back to the USA.

We use the same sauce in different ways: à la Café Brenda in a pasta salad, in mashed potato, as a spoonful stirred into casseroles, and, most regularly, as a superb dip to serve at a finger buffet with roast New Potatoes with Rosemary (see page 109).

Be advised, it is not a sauce for the faint-hearted! If you find the combination of ingredients too strong, try toning down the garlic and chilli. If it's still too strong for you, try something else.

This recipe makes a quantity you won't use all at once, but it freezes well, and will keep for a couple of weeks in the fridge without difficulty.

MAKES ABOUT 900 G (2 LBS)

1 tsp chilli powder
2.5-cm (1-in) slice fresh ginger root, peeled and grated
½ bulb of garlic (4 or 5 cloves), crushed
175 ml (6 fl oz) water
175 g (6 oz) honey
120 ml (4 fl oz) soy sauce
1 jar light tahini
85 ml (3 fl oz) rice wine vinegar (if you have to substitute
another kind of vinegar, use less, as rice wine vinegar is very mild)

1) Put all the ingredients in a blender and whizz until smooth. It may seem rather liquid at first, but it thickens up over time.

Pesto

Fresh, home-made pesto must be one of the most delicious known substances. Its name comes from the Italian word for pestle, because the sauce was traditionally made by pounding together the constituent ingredients with a pestle and mortar. It is based on basil (plus sometimes parsley), garlic and olive oil, thickened with either pine nuts or walnuts, and enriched with either Parmesan or Pecorino. Our version contains these basic ingredients plus lemon juice, which cuts through the richness and helps keep the bright green of the basil. My vote goes strongly for pine nuts over walnuts (they are smoother and creamier) and Parmesan over Pecorino. It is tempting to experiment, varying the herb, the oil, the cheese. We have done a lot of experimenting, but, in most instances, the traditional version of pesto is the best.

Pesto is most often eaten with pasta (see Pasta with Broccoli, Pesto and Cherry Tomatoes, page 73), but it is also delicious with other things. Pesto with mashed potatoes is great (see Special Mashed Potatoes, page 105). Pesto bread (using the method described on pages 16–17 for Celebration Breads) is a great luxury. You can use it in sandwiches or put a spoonful in minestrone or a tomato and red pepper risotto. All these things are luxurious little celebrations made with home-made pesto – with the stuff sold in jars they are a waste of time.

This recipe makes an almost, but not quite, industrial quantity, and has been given this way because it's easier to make in large quantities and keep it than to make it every time you want to use it. To put it in proportion, you'll only need 2 to 3 tablespoonfuls on pasta for a meal for 4 people. Scale down as required, but do use fresh ingredients.

MAKES 1.25 KG (2½ LBS)

4 bunches of basil
2 bunches of flat-leaf parsley
4 good cloves of garlic, peeled
225 g (8 oz) pine nuts
Juice of 2 lemons
50 ml (2 fl oz) water
2 tsp salt
600 ml (1 pint) olive oil
350 g (12 oz) Parmesan, freshly and finely grated

1) Pick over the herbs, discarding all the thick stalks.

2) Put the garlic and pine nuts into a food processor and whizz to a fine powder.

3) Add the lemon juice, water, basil, parsley and salt and whizz until you have a smooth paste.

4) While still whizzing, pour in the olive oil, slowly.

5) Transfer the pesto to a large bowl and stir in the Parmesan. Check the seasoning. Keep in the fridge in an airtight container, ready to use as required.

Harissa

This is a sort of home-made North African curry paste. It is traditionally served with, or stirred into, spicy stews served with couscous. In this book, it features in Aubergine and Chickpea Harissa on page 58, but experiment, stirring this paste into anything you want to spice up. Be careful, though, as it is very hot.

The easiest way to toast the spices is to heat them in a very flat, heavy-bottomed frying pan. They can also be done under the grill or in the oven. Whichever method you use, keep a close eye on them, as they can go from being not done to being burnt rather quickly. They are done when their colour has begun to darken a little and they release their toasty, spicy aroma.

MAKES ABOUT 275 G (10 OZ)

4 tbsp coriander seeds, toasted and ground
2 tbsp cumin seeds, toasted and ground
300 ml (½ pint) olive oil
3 fresh chillies, with seeds
1 bulb of garlic
5-cm (2-in) slice fresh ginger root, peeled

1) Blend all the ingredients in a food processor. Store in a tightly sealed container in the fridge, where it will keep for at least a couple of weeks.

Guacamole

The difference between good and bad guacamole relies on using only ripe and unblemished avocados. The rest, within reason, is a matter of personal taste.

There is a theory that leaving an avocado stone in guacamole stops it from going brown. I am not convinced. I think there are three strategies for avoiding this: not allowing air to get to the purée by putting a layer of clingfilm over the top, putting plenty of lime or lemon juice into it, and eating it fresh.

MAKES 350 G (12 OZ)

Juice of 1 lemon
1 clove of garlic, crushed
Pinch of cayenne pepper
1 tbsp olive oil
½ bunch of coriander, chopped
2 ripe avocados
Salt

1) Prepare all the ingredients, except the avocados and salt, and put them into a blender. When you are ready to whizz it, halve the avocados, remove the stones and peel. Add the avocado flesh to the other ingredients. Whizz and check the seasoning, adding a little salt if necessary.

2) Transfer to a container and lay clingfilm over the surface of the Guacamole, pressing it round the edges. This, with the lemon juice, should prevent it going brown too quickly. Nevertheless, you should eat it on the same day.

Cucumber, Apple and Mint Relish

This is a simple and fragrant relish that is delicious as a light summer chutney with cheeses and vegetable terrines. It also gives a delicious lift to Boston Baked Beans (see page 48) or try it on the side with Roast Shallot and Marjoram Rarebit (see page 130). It is fairly liquid, so don't try to use it in a sandwich!

MAKES ABOUT 450 G (1 LB)

Juice of 2 lemons (or 1½ if very juicy)
50 g (2 oz) caster sugar
1 bunch of mint
2 green apples, cored
½ cucumber, central core of seeds removed

1) Warm the lemon juice and sugar gently in a small pan until the sugar has totally dissolved.

2) Pick the mint leaves from the stalks and chop them very finely. Stir this in to the lemon and sugar syrup.

3) Dice the apples and cucumber very finely. Be sure to put the apple in the lemon syrup as soon as you have cut it so it does not go brown. The appearance of this relish will be greatly enhanced if the apple and cucumber are cut evenly. Stir well. The relish is now ready. If not using immediately, store in the fridge, but, in any event, do not keep it for more than 3 or 4 days.

Onion Marmalade

When I have my thatched pub in the country with roses growing round the door and I make my own cheese, I will serve this 'marmalade' as part of the best ploughman's lunch in Britain. Until then, I shall dream and enjoy it with toasted cheese, warmed goats' cheese or the Lentil, Leek and Parmesan Bake (see page 87).

MAKES ABOUT 350 G (12 OZ)

50 ml (2 fl oz) olive oil
750 g (1½ lbs) onions, halved and finely sliced
2 tbsp balsamic vinegar
1 tbsp molasses sugar
½ tsp salt

1) In a heavy-bottomed pan, heat the oil. Add the onions and fry over a high heat for about 20 minutes, stirring every 2 to 3 minutes so that the onions brown in between stirrings but do not burn.

2) Add the vinegar, sugar and salt and cook fiercely for a minute. Take off the heat. Taste and adjust the salt, sugar and vinegar to your taste. This will keep well in the fridge for a few days, but be sure to allow it to come up to room temperature before serving.

Vinaigrette

We use lots of this dressing every day at the restaurant. I like plenty of mustard and a high proportion of decent olive oil to vinegar in a vinaigrette.

You get the best result if you make this in a blender or food processor, but it can be done perfectly well by hand. The recipe makes a fairly large quantity, but keeps for weeks in the fridge.

MAKES 600 ML (1 PINT)

1 bunch of fresh herb of your choice (we usually use dill, but parsley or mint are also good)
85 ml (3 fl oz) white wine vinegar
1 tbsp coarse-grain mustard
½ tsp salt
450 ml (15 fl oz) olive oil

1) Discard any tough herb stalks.

2) Put the herb, vinegar, mustard and salt in the food processor and whizz. While still whizzing, slowly pour in the olive oil – the dressing should emulsify. Check the seasoning and add salt to taste. If you like a sweeter taste, add a little sugar or honey.

Honey and Ginger Dressing

This makes a rich, sweet and creamy dressing – especially good on salads containing fruit.

MAKES 450 ML (¾ PINT)

1 clove of garlic, crushed
1 piece of stem ginger
50 ml (2 fl oz) white wine vinegar
2 tbsp tahini
1 tbsp honey
300 ml (½ pint) sunflower oil
Salt

1) Put the garlic, ginger and vinegar into a food processor and whizz until smooth.

2) Add the tahini and honey and whizz again. While still whizzing, slowly pour in the sunflower oil. The dressing will thicken; if it gets too thick, add a little water. Add salt to taste.

Rich Dill Dressing

I am generally very suspicious of vegetarian 'substitutes' for traditional ingredients (veggie burgers, sausages, mince, steak and so on I have always found to be horrible), but, nevertheless, I have come to prefer rich emulsions made with silken tofu to traditional egg mayonnaise. So, give this a try before you creep away at the mention of the word tofu.

It's especially delicious with any salads using sea vegetables, and is also delicious with vegetable sushi (try asparagus). Made with garlic and chives instead of dill, it makes a good dressing for new potatoes. Try it also as a dipping sauce for globe artichokes.

You can sometimes find silken tofu in supermarkets, but it is easily available in healthfood shops. Firm tofu will not work for this dressing.

MAKES 300 ML (½ PINT)

1 bunch of dill, any tough stalks removed
½ clove of garlic, crushed
Juice of 1 lemon
1 tsp honey
1 tsp soy sauce
1 packet silken tofu
1 tsp French mustard (not the grainy sort)
½ tsp salt
50 ml (2 fl oz) olive oil

1) Put all the ingredients, except the oil, into a food processor and whizz until smooth.

2) While still whizzing, add the olive oil. Taste and adjust the seasoning if necessary.

Tomato Sauce

This is a good basic tomato sauce, fine on pasta. It can be used as an alternative sauce on Lentil, Leek and Parmesan Bake (see page 87).

If you can get good, ripe, fresh plum tomatoes, so much the better, but using tinned plum tomatoes (not the ready chopped versions, which are not necessarily plum tomatoes and can taste more acidic) is the best bet for most people in the UK most of the time.

MAKES 600 ML (1 PINT)

1 medium onion, finely chopped
1 clove of garlic, crushed
50 ml (2 fl oz) olive oil
1 x 400-g (14-oz) tin plum tomatoes, liquidized
1 bunch of basil, finely chopped
salt and freshly ground black pepper

1) Sweat the onion and garlic in the olive oil for at least 15 minutes, until very soft.

2) Add the tomatoes and bring to the boil. Simmer, uncovered, for at least 15 minutes.

3) Stir in the basil and season to taste with salt and pepper.

Roast Marinated Tofu

For many years, I was a confirmed tofu-hater. I neither liked it in slimy bits in healthfood café stews, nor in rubber cubes in stir-fries in Chinese restaurants. My road to Damascus was in Sarah Brown's kitchen, when I nibbled idly at some crisp brown squares she had made while preparing for a cookery demonstration. They were moreish in the way that Sour Cream and Chive Pringles are moreish – savoury and mouth-watering. I'm not sure if I left her any for the demonstration!

Since then, we have made our version of marinated and roast tofu many times at The Place Below – I have even demonstrated the British way of cooking tofu on Japanese TV!

We serve it stirred into Guinness and Mushroom Casserole (see pages 38–9 – do this just before you are going to eat or it will go slimy), on salads with garlicky roast field mushrooms or as part of a little kebab, with squares of roast pepper or Italian baby onions pickled in balsamic vinegar.

The first time you use the marinade, it will only take about 2 hours for the tofu to take on its flavour and colour, but it gets weaker with use. If you re-use it a couple of times, you will need to leave the tofu in overnight for it to absorb sufficient flavour. Don't use it more than 4 times in any event. You will probably find that you have used any leftover marinade in sauces long before you want to use it as a marinade for the fourth time anyway.

Note that silken tofu will not work for this recipe. Firm tofu is now generally available in most supermarkets and healthfood stores.

MAKES 16 BITE-SIZED PIECES

250 g (9 oz) firm tofu, cubed
50 ml (2 fl oz) soy sauce
50 ml (2 fl oz) red wine
50 ml (2 fl oz) water
1 clove of garlic, crushed
2.5-cm (1-in) slice fresh ginger root, peeled and chopped
2 tbsp sesame oil
1 tsp Tabasco sauce

1) Put the tofu cubes into a bowl. Mix together the marinade ingredients – the soy sauce, wine, water, garlic and ginger – and pour it over the tofu. Leave for at least 2 hours (see note above). If the marinade does not quite cover the tofu, either add a bit more wine and soy sauce or else turn the tofu every so often so that it gets evenly doused.

2) When the tofu is ready, pre-heat the oven to 220°C/425°F/Gas 7.

3) Take the tofu out of the marinade and place the cubes apart on a baking sheet. (The marinade should be stored in the fridge in an airtight container to use again.) Mix the sesame oil and Tabasco and pour over the tofu. Turn the cubes over with a spoon until the tofu is evenly coated. Bake in the pre-heated oven for 40 minutes to 1 hour, until the cubes are crisp all over. I like the tofu to be very crisp, but some people prefer it a little softer – try it both ways and see which you like best.

CHAPTER 10

Bill's Snacks

Roast Shallot and Marjoram Rarebit

Beans on Toast à la Bill

Scrambled Duck Eggs on Field Mushrooms

Quick Stuffed Peppers

Asparagus, New Potatoes, Wilted Spinach and Rocket with Pecorino

Tagliatelle with Asparagus and Tarragon

Beef Tomatoes with Goats' Cheese, Olive Oil and Herbs

Ines' Spanish Omelette

Roast Shallot and Marjoram Rarebit

In my not remotely vegetarian childhood, toasted cheese was invariably used by my mother to create instant contentment among fractious and hungry children. Sarah and I still regularly turn to this simplest of comfort foods, sometimes creating greater levels of sophistication by adding mango chutney or grilled tomatoes.

This luxurious and simple supper snack is barely any more complicated than that. It is given an extra lift by the fresh marjoram (a close relative of oregano). It's delicious. Serve with Cucumber, Apple and Mint Relish (see page 121) or just a plain apple.

SERVES 2

175 g (6 oz) small shallots
2 tbsp sunflower oil
Salt and freshly ground black pepper
100 g (4 oz) strong Cheddar, grated
1 tsp grainy mustard
2 tbsp Guinness
15 g (½ oz) butter
½ bunch of marjoram, roughly chopped
2 slices of bread (Place Below Daily Bread, pages 14–15, is great for this)

1) Pre-heat the oven to 220°C/425°F/Gas 7.

2) Peel the shallots and put them on a baking sheet. Pour the oil over them, mix them thoroughly in it to coat and season well. Bake in the pre-heated oven for about 20 minutes, until the shallots are browning on the outside and tender.

3) Meanwhile, place the remaining ingredients (except the bread) in a small pan and heat gently until the mixture is thick and creamy. Stir in the roast shallots.

4) Toast the bread. Place on the grillpan and pour the cheesy mixture over them. Cook under a hot grill until the topping is golden and bubbling.

Beans on Toast à la Bill

I love baked beans on toast. I'm not talking about home-made Boston Baked Beans here (see page 48), but plain, ordinary tinned baked beans, made by you know who. Well, plain, ordinary tinned beans with two vital additions.

You want to use a good strong cheese – I suggest Gruyère, cut off a round cheese (the stuff cut off a square block is not nearly so good). Our wonderful local cheese shop in London, Vivian's, sells a French cheese called Comté, which is quite similar and equally delicious.

SERVES 2

1 x 420-g (15-oz) tin baked beans
4 slices of bread (Place Below Daily Bread, pages 14–15, is excellent for this)
Knob of butter
½ tsp Marmite
50 g (2 oz) Gruyère cheese, grated

1) Open the tin of beans and pour them into a saucepan. Heat gently, stirring occasionally, until the beans are piping hot.

2) Toast the bread and spread with the butter and a little Marmite.

3) Stir the grated Gruyère into the hot baked beans and pour over the toast.

Scrambled Duck Eggs on Field Mushrooms

OK, so you can't always find duck eggs in your local shop or supermarket and, yes, you can make this perfectly well with hens' eggs. However, the first time I did this, I made it with duck eggs (a present from a visiting uncle-in-law) and it was so rich and delicious (they have a higher proportion of yolk to white than hens' eggs), I think it's worth at least keeping your eyes open for duck eggs.

These make superb appetizers using small mushrooms (give your guests bibs) or, with bigger field mushrooms, are a great example of what Simon Hopkinson of Bibendum calls 'SSF' – Sunday supper food – even though there is no toast.

SERVES 2 FOR SUPPER OR 6 AS A PRE-DINNER TITBIT

3 tbsp olive oil
1 clove of garlic, crushed
1 tbsp soy sauce
6 big field or 12 small mushrooms
3 eggs (preferably duck eggs)
50 ml (2 fl oz) single cream
25 g (1 oz) butter
1 bunch of chives, chopped
Salt and freshly ground black pepper

1) Pre-heat the oven to 200°C/400°F/Gas 6.

2) Mix the oil, garlic and soy sauce together.

3) Arrange the mushrooms in a baking dish with the gills upwards. Brush them with the oil mixture, using it all up. Bake in the pre-heated oven for 10 to 15 minutes, until just becoming tender. Remove from the oven and leave to one side.

4) Lightly beat the eggs and mix in the cream.

5) Melt the butter in a small, heavy-bottomed pan over a low heat. Add the egg mixture and keep stirring. When nearly done (I like it still fairly liquid, but this is a matter of taste), take the pan off the heat, add the chives, taste and season generously with salt and pepper. Dollop on to the mushrooms and eat.

Quick Stuffed Peppers

Use one red and one yellow pepper for visual effect; don't use green ones.

SERVES 2

2 large peppers, halved lengthways and deseeded
1 courgette, finely chopped
2 fresh, ripe, plum tomatoes, finely chopped
75 g (3 oz) pesto (preferably home-made, see pages 117–18)
75 g (3 oz) ricotta
Salt and freshly ground black pepper
4 small pieces of white bread
2 tbsp olive oil

1) Pre-heat the oven to 200°C/400°F/Gas 6.

2) Grease a baking dish and lay the pepper halves in it.

3) Mix the courgette, tomatoes, pesto and ricotta. Check the seasoning and add salt to taste (it may need more than you expect, as ricotta is fairly bland).

4) Fill each half pepper with the mixture and put a piece of bread on top of each. Brush with olive oil with a little salt and pepper in it.

5) Bake in the pre-heated oven for about 30 minutes, until the toast is golden brown.

Asparagus, New Potatoes,
Wilted Spinach and Rocket with Pecorino

Asparagus is expensive, even during its short domestic season, but it is also quick to prepare and cook, and tastes and looks beautiful. That is why it features in two recipes in this chapter. For both of them I use medium-sized asparagus; if you use the real jumbo grade, you will only get about two bits each (and, anyway, it probably comes from California and is several days old) and sprue asparagus is somehow too small to make a proper mouthful.

This dish is half-way between a salad and a hot dish. If you're feeling really extravagant, use Jersey Royal new potatoes as their season happily overlaps with that of English asparagus.

SERVES 4

750 g (1½ lbs) new potatoes
450 g (1 lb) asparagus
50 ml (2 fl oz) olive oil
225 g (8 oz) fresh baby spinach, washed
25 g (1 oz) rocket, washed
Salt and freshly ground black pepper
100 g (4 oz) Pecorino

1) Boil the new potatoes in plenty of salted water until just cooked, drain and set aside. (Different potatoes take different lengths of time to cook, so keep testing and be careful not to overcook them.)

2) Snap the woody ends off the asparagus. (This is a Delia tip – if you bend a bit of asparagus, it magically snaps at the point where it becomes unpleasantly woody.) Boil in plenty of salted water for 3 to 5 minutes, until just cooked. (Some people recommend boiling asparagus for much longer – up to 10 to 12 minutes – but for me it then loses all its texture and fresh taste.)

3) Have ready a large frying pan. Heat the olive oil and, when hot, add the potatoes and fry for for about 5 minutes. Add the spinach and rocket and turn in the hot oil for a few seconds until it is just beginning to wilt. Season with salt and pepper to taste.

4) Divide between 4 plates and decorate with the asparagus. Garnish with a generous quantity of Pecorino shavings (if you can only get hold of young Pecorino, though, you may find you have to crumble it rather than shave it). Eat at once.

Tagliatelle with Asparagus and Tarragon

Decent pasta tossed in olive oil, seasoned with salt and freshly ground black pepper and served with freshly grated Parmesan and a salad of Baby Gem lettuce makes our favourite quick supper at home. There are innumerable variations on this theme, the key point being that you don't have to make a sauce, which is the time-consuming thing about making more complicated pasta recipes. Add some finely chopped artichoke hearts or sun-dried tomatoes preserved in oil, some roast or grilled peppers, some quickly fried fennel or courgettes or some ripe, raw, fresh tomatoes and fresh basil. In all cases, toss the pasta in sufficient decent olive oil to make it slippery and fragrant to eat. You can also vary the cheese – Pecorino is another favourite, and really mature Cheddar is also good (even if it is less authentic).

Asparagus blanched and tossed in hot butter with fresh tarragon makes a superb and incredibly easy starter. This recipe combines this idea with the quick pasta dish described above. The use of both olive oil *and* butter is, perhaps, a little decadent, but it is delicious.

You can buy excellent pasta – both fresh and dried – in most supermarkets now. My preference for this dish is a fresh, egg-based tagliatelle. I also love the very fine pasta, *paglia e fieno*.

For the quickest and simplest way to make this dish, you want to buy medium-thick asparagus, which takes 4 to 5 minutes to cook, and a tagliatelle that also takes 4 to 5 minutes to cook. If the pasta you are using takes a different length of time to cook (the instructions for timing on pasta packets I have generally found to be extremely reliable, so long as you use a large pan with plenty of boiling water), then put it in the pan the appropriate number of minutes before or after the asparagus. They can still share the same pan of boiling water.

SERVES 2

225 g (8 oz) fresh tagliatelle
225 g (8 oz) asparagus, woody ends snapped off (see page 134)
50 ml (2 fl oz) olive oil
25 g (1 oz) butter
½ bunch of tarragon, leaves stripped from the stalks
Salt and freshly ground black pepper
50 g (2 oz) Parmesan, freshly and coarsely grated

1) Bring a large pan of salted water to the boil. Add the tagliatelle and asparagus together (but see the notes above about cooking times of the pasta) and boil for 4 to 5 minutes, until both are just cooked. Drain them both together.

2) In the emptied pan, heat the olive oil and butter, then add the tarragon and some salt and pepper. Return the pasta and asparagus to the pan, together with half the Parmesan. Mix thoroughly (tongs are the best tool for doing this). Serve immediately with remaining Parmesan sprinkled over.

Beef Tomatoes with
Goats' Cheese, Olive Oil and Herbs

For this dish, you need a mature, meltable goats' cheese. When testing this recipe in Cornwall, I used a local 'Nanny's Cheddar', which worked very well.

To make the breadcrumbs quickly, put a couple of slices of bread in the food processor and whizz until they become crumbs.

SERVES 2

2 large beef tomatoes
50 g (2 oz) fresh breadcrumbs
50 g (2 oz) goats' cheese, finely chopped or grated depending on type
1 tbsp chopped stoned olives
2 sprigs of fresh thyme
2 tbsp olive oil

1) Pre-heat the oven to 220°C/425°F/Gas 7.

2) Cut the tops off the tomatoes and reserve. Scrape out the insides of the tomatoes into a mixing bowl, discarding any hard bits of the core. Mix with half the breadcrumbs and all the rest of the ingredients.

3) Put the mixture back into the tomatoes, sprinkle the rest of the breadcrumbs on top and then put the reserved tomato 'lids' back on. Put the stuffed tomatoes into a small ovenproof dish that has been lightly brushed with olive oil and bake in the pre-heated oven for 15 minutes, until bubbling and the tomatoes are beginning to look wrinkled.

Ines' Spanish Omelette

When you have grown up with a particular kind of food, you understand it in a way that it is difficult to learn as an adult. Ines cooked at The Place Below for about four years and, during that time, we often had Spanish omelette on the menu and it was always delicious. Since she left to have her second child, we have not served it once. However, cooked in a small quantity at home, it is simple and just the sort of restorative food you need after a stressful day. When testing Ines' at home, we ate it with a salad of baby spinach, broccoli and roast peppers with a mint and garlic dressing – a great combination.

Once again, don't skimp on the olive oil – if you want to reduce your fat intake, simply eat less of the omelette. If you don't have fresh thyme, parsley or mint are also good. It may seem like you're creating unnecessary washing-up using two frying pans to make this, but you need a big one for frying the onions and potatoes, and the omelette would be too shallow if you used the same one for cooking the final mixture.

SERVES 2

85 ml (3 fl oz) olive oil
225 g (8 oz) red onions, halved and thinly sliced
225 g (8 oz) potatoes, halved and very thinly sliced
Salt and freshly ground black pepper
3 eggs
½ bunch of fresh thyme, leaves picked from the stalks

1) In a large, heavy-bottomed frying pan, heat two thirds of the olive oil. Add the onions and fry over a medium heat for about 5 minutes, until they are beginning to soften.

2) Add the potato slices and some salt and pepper and continue to fry, stirring regularly, until the potatoes are just cooked. Remove from the heat.

3) In a mixing bowl, mix the eggs with some more salt and pepper and the fresh thyme. Stir in the cooked onions and potatoes and any juices from the pan.

4) Heat the remaining oil in a small (20-cm/8-in diameter by 2.5-cm/1-in deep), heavy-bottomed frying pan. Pour in the mixture and turn down to the lowest heat. Meanwhile, pre-heat the grill to its highest temperature. When the bottom of the omelette is set but the top bit is still liquid (about 10 minutes), put the pan under the grill for 1 to 2 minutes, just to set the top (this is considerably easier than turning the omelette over and then cooking the other side in the pan). Turn the omelette out on to a plate and serve it.

CHAPTER 11

Tarts and Puddings

Apple, Pear and Almond Crumble

Summer Pudding

Treacle Sponge Pudding

Brioche, Orange and Marmalade Pudding

Simple and Perfect Sweet Pastry

Lemon and Almond Tart

Prune and Brandy Tart

Pecan Pie

Apple and Lemon Tart

Chocolate and Prune Tart

Pear and Almond Tart

Rhubarb and Strawberry Compote

Apple, Pear and Almond Crumble

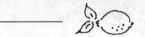

If I were marooned on a desert island with a British climate and I was only allowed to eat one pudding, it would, without any doubt, be Place Below Apple, Pear and Almond Crumble.

In the first few days after I opened the restaurant in 1989, there were two things I was determined that we would never serve – quiche and crumble. None of that homespun nonsense, we were going to be a sophisticated restaurant. Customer demand put paid to my quiche prejudice and my mother overcame my post-nouvelle cuisine anti-crumble line. She had no comprehension of my misguided food snobbery, particularly as she had fed us almost no other pudding as children (until she discovered Marks and Spencers' fruit fools). When you have tried this rich and fruity concoction – preferably served with clotted cream, I'm sure you will agree that 'Mum knows best'.

We don't peel either the apples or the pears, but whether or not you want to is a matter of personal taste.

There are, of course, endless possible variations on this recipe. The one I was most surprised to enjoy was apple and strawberry. Whichever fruit you choose (rhubarb, gooseberry, nectarine, redcurrant are all delicious) combine it with a slightly greater weight of apples.

SERVES 6–8

FOR THE APPLE AND PEAR FILLING

900 g (2 lbs) cooking apples
15 g (½ oz) unsalted butter
50 ml (2 fl oz) apple juice
75 g (3 oz) demerara sugar
750 g (1½ lbs) pears, cored and roughly diced
100 g (4 oz) raisins (preferably Lexia)

FOR THE CRUMBLE TOPPING

100 g (4 oz) plain wholemeal flour
50 g (2 oz) demerara sugar
50 g (2 oz) unsalted butter
50 g (2 oz) ground almonds
A few whole almonds, to decorate

1) Pre-heat the oven to 220°C/425°F/Gas 7.

2) To make the filling, core and chop the apples and put the pieces in a pan with the butter, apple juice and sugar, then bring to the boil. Cover and simmer for about 15 minutes. When the apples are quite tender, take the pan off the heat and stir in the pears and raisins. If the pears are very hard, put them in the apple mix half way through its cooking time.

3) To make the crumble topping, put the flour, sugar, butter and ground almonds into a food processor and whizz briefly until the mixture looks like breadcrumbs.

4) Pour the fruit mixture into a baking dish about 22 by 15 cm (9 by 6 in) and cover evenly with the crumble mix. Decorate with the whole almonds and bake in the pre-heated oven for about 25 to 30 minutes, until it is turning golden on top.

Summer Pudding

How can anyone say there is no tradition of great food in Britain when we have summer pudding? It makes use of the summer berries, which flourish in our climate, and it brings out their best qualities without unduly messing them around (just the characteristics we are always raving on about being so brilliant in Mediterranean cooking). Moreover, in case you are concerned about such things, it contains virtually no fat and is vegan – unless of course you eat it, as I often do, with clotted cream.

You can vary the proportions and types of fruit used, but maintaining a balance between the more tart currants and the sweeter fruit such as strawberries is important. Remember that if you do use a smaller proportion of currants, then you should cut down on the quantity of sugar used. Using frozen blackcurrants and redcurrants works perfectly well, but if you make it with frozen raspberries or strawberries, the result is nowhere near as good as when you use fresh ones.

The use of factory-made sliced white bread is also important. Summer pudding made with wholemeal bread is one of those well-meaning ideas (like wholemeal pasta but unlike really good wholemeal pastry) that you think may be a great development, but, in fact, does not taste right at all!

SERVES 8

350 g (12 oz) blackcurrants
350 g (12 oz) redcurrants
175 g (6 oz) caster sugar
450 g (1 lb) raspberries
450 g (1 lb) strawberries, hulled and halved
1 medium-cut sliced white loaf

1) Warm the currants with the sugar in a pan over a very low heat until the sugar has dissolved in their juice. Drain the fruit, keeping the juice. Mix the barely cooked currants with the raspberries and strawberries.

2) Remove the crusts from the bread. Briefly dip the pieces of bread in the reserved fruit juice and, after each one has been dipped, use it to line a 2.3-litre (4-pint) pudding basin. There should be no white patches of bread and it should go about three quarters of the way up the sides of the basin. Make sure, too, that there are no gaps between the bits of bread or the pudding will collapse more easily when you unmould it.

3) Fill the lined basin with the fruit. Make a top with more dipped bread – again ensuring that there are no holes in it. There should be just enough juice to dip all the bits of bread into. Put a plate on top of the pudding. Weigh down and leave on a tray in the fridge overnight.

4) Next day, remove weights and plate, turn out carefully and serve.

Treacle Sponge Pudding

Located as we are in the heart of London's financial district, those under 18 make up a tiny proportion of our customers, so I feel doubly proud that my cousin-in-law, Gemma Green (aged 12 at the time of writing), reckons that this is her favourite pudding. It is mouth-watering comfort food.

This recipe makes 16 medium-sized portions, which sounds a lot but they will disappear quickly (so Gemma tells me). If you are eating it as a cake rather than a pudding, then serve it at room temperature and leave out the sauce.

SERVES 16

FOR THE CAKE

225 g (8 oz) stoned prunes
225 g (8 oz) soft brown sugar
250 ml (8 fl oz) sunflower oil
4 eggs
275 g (10 oz) plain flour
1 tsp bicarbonate of soda
3 tsp cinnamon
1 tsp ground ginger
1 tsp ground nutmeg
250 ml (8 fl oz) milk

FOR THE TOPPING

100 g (4 oz) soft brown sugar
85 ml (3 fl oz) milk
2 tbsp molasses

FOR THE SAUCE

75 g (3 oz) unsalted butter
225 g (8 oz) soft brown sugar
150 ml (¼ pint) double cream
2 tbsp molasses

1) Pre-heat the oven to 180°C/350°F/Gas 4.

2) To make the cake, put the prunes into a small saucepan. Just cover them with water and bring to the boil. Simmer for 10 to 15 minutes, until tender and the water has been absorbed. Chop them roughly. (If you can't get hold of stoned prunes, then cook them before removing the stones – it's much easier.)

3) Whisk together the sugar, oil and eggs until you have a thick, smooth mixture.

4) Fold in the flour, bicarbonate of soda and spices. Mix well.

5) Add the prunes and milk and mix. Pour the batter into a lined 28 by 20 by 4-cm (11 by 8 by 1½-in) tin and bake in the pre-heated oven for 30 minutes, until risen, golden and it will spring back when lightly pressed in the centre.

6) While the cake is baking, warm the ingredients for the topping together. When the cake is ready, prick the top and pour the topping over.

7) Next, make the sauce. Put all the ingredients into a pan and heat gently until hot.

8) To serve, place the required number of portions of cake in a grill pan, pour some sauce over and grill until bubbling hot, then serve immediately.

Brioche, Orange and Marmalade Pudding

This is about as rich a bread and butter pudding as you could imagine, especially if you make it with the Brioche on pages 19–20, which contains considerably more butter than most shop-bought brioche. However, the marmalade, the fresh orange segments and the splash of whisky bring balance and luxury to Frances' delicious recipe. (Just make sure you don't serve it after a main course that is full of butter, eggs and cream.) You could also try it with pears and redcurrant sauce; it does need some acidity to balance the richness of the pudding.

SERVES 8

350 g (12 oz) brioche
150 g (5 oz) unsalted butter
225 g (8 oz) marmalade
2 tbsp whisky
3 oranges, segmented (i.e. with all the pith removed)
3 eggs
100 g (4 oz) light muscovado sugar
450 ml (¾ pint) single cream
Zest of 1 orange
3 tbsp demerara sugar

1) Pre-heat the oven to 180°C/350°F/Gas 4.

2) Roughly break the brioche into a baking dish 22 by 15 cm (9 by 6 in).

3) Melt the butter and pour it over the brioche. Melt the marmalade with the whisky over a low heat, then pour this over the brioche and butter and stir it all around a bit.

4) Add the orange segments and mix carefully again.

5) To make the custard, lightly whisk the eggs, sugar, cream and orange zest and pour over the brioche. Sprinkle the demerara sugar on top.

6) Bake the pudding in the pre-heated oven for about 1 hour, until just set. Note that it will continue to cook slightly when out of the oven.

Simple and Perfect Sweet Pastry

We make a lot of sweet tarts at The Place Below. I think that there is nothing more mouthwatering than a freshly glazed fruit tart, a chocolate tart dusted with icing sugar or the delicate yellow of a fresh lemon tart. All of them rely on a decent sweet pastry.

I was very briefly a vegetable commis chef (the lowest of the low) at the excellent Launceston Place restaurant in Kensington, London, and, after my second week, the French pastry chef announced that he was leaving in two days' time. I was therefore given two days to learn those bits of his art that featured on the current menu, and this sweet pastry was one of his recipes.

In a food processor, it is very simple to make. It is also easy to work with, so long as it is thoroughly chilled before you try to roll it out. If it has become totally hard in the fridge, just knead it a little before starting to roll.

Even if you only plan to make one tart, I strongly recommend that you make a larger batch of pastry if you have a reasonably large food processor. Then simply divide it into three (if you are following the recipes in this book which are all written for a 23-cm/9-in tin), wrap them in clingfilm and freeze the two you are not going to use immediately. Put the one for immediate use in the fridge and chill for at least an hour.

MAKES SUFFICIENT FOR THREE 23-CM (9-IN) OR TWO 30-CM (12-IN) TARTS

200 g (7 oz) unsalted butter, cut into small pieces
350 g (12 oz) plain white flour
75 g (3 oz) caster sugar
2 size 3 eggs, lightly beaten

1) Whizz the butter and flour together in a food processor. Otherwise, rub the butter into the flour with the tips of your fingers, lifting the mixture as you do so, until it looks like breadcrumbs.

2) Add the sugar and whizz again or, if making by hand, rub the sugar in, too.

3) Add the eggs and whizz again or mix them in thoroughly to gather the crumbs together into a dough. Divide the dough into 3 equal-sized pieces, cover in clingfilm and chill thoroughly before using.

4) See page 67 for how to make pastry cases and bake them blind.

Lemon and Almond Tart

There are more lemon tart recipes floating around London restaurants than many foodies have had hot dinners. For me, the key element is that the lemon flavour should be strong and fresh – not simply a custard with a hint of lemon. We have regularly made two contrasting lemon tarts. We started off with a fresh lemon curd tart with a deliciously smooth texture, but, more recently, have been seduced by this perfectly balanced almond-based tart.

The best tool for getting the zest from the lemon is the fine part of a hand-held grater, which is held over the bowl with the juice in. You want to get the oil which sprays from the lemon as you grate and you do not want great long strands of lemon peel which you get using a so-called lemon zester.

SERVES 8

2 *eggs*
150 g (5 oz) icing sugar, plus extra for dusting
Juice and zest of 4 lemons
90 g (3½ oz) butter, melted
65 g (2½ oz) ground almonds
1 x 23-cm (9-in) sweet pastry case, baked blind (see pages 147 and 67)

1) Pre-heat oven to 180°C/350°F/Gas 4.

2) Beat the eggs and icing sugar together until fluffy.

3) Mix in the rest of the ingredients. Don't panic if the mixture curdles at this point; the tart will still be fine.

4) Pour the lemony mixture into the pastry case and bake in the pre-heated oven for 25 minutes, until the filling has set and is just beginning to turn golden on top. Allow to cool and serve at room temperature, dusted with icing sugar.

Prune and Brandy Tart

It is a terrible truth that this tart does not sell as well as other puddings, although everyone who tries it loves it. British people have this thing about prunes – or, rather, about childhood memories of prunes. My Dad would look up apologetically from his morning plate of tinned prunes and All-Bran and explain what effective medicine it was. If you have such memories, rewind your brain and press the erase button.

Prunes are delicious and we should *enjoy* their dense, sweet luxury, as they do in France, where they are more likely to be paired with Armagnac than bran. The best varieties are either the superb pruneaux d'Agen or the plump Californians.

Serve this tart either plain or with crème anglaise (proper custard) or cream flavoured with brandy.

SERVES 8

225 g (8 oz) stoned prunes
60 ml (2 fl oz), plus 1 tbsp, brandy
75 g (3 oz) unsalted butter
75 g (3 oz) caster sugar
2 eggs, beaten
50 g (2 oz) ground almonds
1 x 23-cm (9-in) sweet pastry case, baked blind (see pages 147 and 67)
2 tbsp apricot jam

1) Pre-heat the oven to 180°C/350°F/Gas 4.

2) Soak the prunes in the 60 ml (2 fl oz) of brandy overnight.

3) Cream together the butter and sugar in a food processor or in a bowl. Gradually add in the beaten eggs. Then, add the ground almonds and mix again. Mix in any brandy not absorbed by the prunes.

4) Arrange the soaked prunes in the pastry case, pour the almond mixture over them and bake in the pre-heated oven for about 30 minutes, until the filling has set.

5) Glaze with the apricot jam, heated with the remaining brandy mixed into it. Serve warm or at room temperature.

Pecan Pie

This is Ian's version of the classic American recipe. It is fairly expensive, but it isn't as good if you substitute cheaper ingredients, such as golden syrup for maple, or walnuts for pecan nuts.

Serve it with clotted cream to ensure complete happiness.

SERVES 8

175 g (6 oz) demerara sugar
175 ml (6 fl oz) real maple syrup (check the bottle carefully)
2 eggs
1 tbsp milk
50 g (2 oz) unsalted butter, softened
225 g (8 oz) pecan nuts, shelled
1 x 23-cm (9-in) sweet pastry case, baked blind (see pages 147 and 67)

1) Pre-heat the oven to 190°C/375°F/Gas 5.

2) Boil the sugar and syrup together for 3 minutes.

3) Whisk the eggs and milk together. While still whisking, pour in the sugar and syrup mixture.

4) Pour this mixture back into the saucepan and cook over a *very low heat* until it thickens slightly. Unless you allow it to thicken a little, it will seek out the invisible cracks in your perfect pastry case and leak all over your oven! *Stir all the time with a wooden spoon.*

5) Stir in the butter and pecan nuts.

6) Pour the filling into the pastry case and bake in the pre-heated oven for about 30 minutes, until the filling has set and browned slightly. Serve at room temperature.

Apple and Lemon Tart

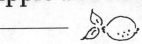

This is a lovely, fresh tart in which the apples are strongly flavoured with lemon. Either Cox's or Russets in season are good for this.

SERVES 8

900 g (2 lbs) eating apples, unpeeled, 675 g (1½ lbs) grated,
225 g (½ lb) cored and thinly sliced
Juice and zest of 2 lemons
100 g (4 oz) demerara sugar
1 x 23-cm (9-in) sweet pastry case, baked blind (see pages 147 and 67)
50 g (2 oz) apricot jam (optional)

1) Pre-heat the oven to 220°C/425°F/Gas 7.

2) Mix the grated apples with the lemon juice, zest and sugar. Place in a colander on a plate to catch the juice and drain well.

3) Spread the drained grated mix in the pastry case, then arrange the apple slices neatly on top in overlapping circles.

4) Bake in the pre-heated oven for 40 minutes.

5) Meanwhile, reduce the reserved juice to use to glaze the tart. Alternatively, heat the apricot jam and use this once the tart is cooked.

Chocolate and Prune Tart

This is a relative newcomer to our repertoire and I think it is delicious. The thin coating of prune purée underneath the lightly cooked chocolate mousse provides a fruity edge to contrast with the richness of the mousse.

You can find excellent French prune purée in jars at good delicatessens, but it's also very simple to make your own, as described here.

Serve this tart barely warm with pouring cream.

SERVES 8

FOR THE PRUNE PURÉE

75 g (3 oz) stoned prunes
50 ml (2 fl oz) apple juice
1 tbsp brandy

FOR THE CHOCOLATE MOUSSE

100 g (4 oz) unsalted butter
100 g (4 oz) good-quality plain chocolate
1 egg
3 egg yolks
25 g (1 oz) caster sugar

1 x 23-cm (9-in) sweet pastry case, baked blind (see pages 147 and 67)

1) Pre-heat the oven to 190°C/375°F/Gas 5.

2) To make the prune purée, place the prunes in a pan with the apple juice. Bring to the boil, then simmer gently, covered, for about 20 minutes, until the prunes are tender and the liquid has virtually all been absorbed. Purée in a blender, adding the brandy. The resulting purée should be the consistency of jam.

3) To make the chocolate mousse, melt the butter in a pan over a low heat. Break the chocolate up a bit and melt it into the butter.

4) In a bowl, whisk the egg and egg yolks with the sugar until the mixture will leave a trail when the whisk is lifted. Fold it into the chocolate and butter mix (off the heat).

5) Spread the prune purée evenly over the bottom of the pastry case. Then, spread the chocolate mousse mixture evenly on top of it. Bake in the pre-heated oven for 15 minutes. There should be a thin crust on top, but the mixture should still be mousse-like underneath.

Pear and Almond Tart

As with lemon tarts, so with pear and almond (or frangipane as the almond mixture is known) – there is no limit to the number of different recipes.

When Sarah and I were in Cornwall testing these recipes, our landlords invited us to dinner and served a similarly delicious recipe, but topped with Amaretti biscuits soaked in brandy. I loved the hit of brandy this gave, so I have included this as an optional extra.

Many kinds of fruit can be used with this almond mixture. Nectarines and peaches are delicious. Quinces are good, but need pre-cooking. I also love this recipe made with soft fruit, such as raspberries or redcurrants – their juice bursts into the frangipane while cooking and the whole thing turns a lovely murky pink colour.

If you are using pears that are really unripe, prepare them as instructed and then poach the pieces in some apple juice before arranging them in the pastry case.

The tart is best served slightly warm rather than hot.

SERVES 8

2 size 1 eggs
100 g (4 oz) unsalted butter, softened
100 g (4 oz) caster sugar
½ tsp almond essence
100 g (4 oz) ground almonds
40 g (1½ oz) plain flour
½ tsp baking powder
2 medium pears, cored and quartered (peeling optional)
1 x 23-cm (9-in) sweet pastry case, baked blind (see pages 147 and 67)
9 Amaretti biscuits and 60 ml (2 fl oz) brandy (optional)
50 g (2 oz) apricot jam

1) Pre-heat the oven to 190°C/375°F/Gas 5.

2) Whizz the eggs, butter, sugar, almond essence, almonds, flour and baking powder together in a food processor until the mixture becomes pale. This is the frangipane.

3) Arrange the pears in pastry case and spread the frangipane mixture over them.

4) If using the optional topping, soak the Amaretti biscuits in the brandy and arrange them on top, 8 in a circle around the edge and 1 in the middle. Any surplus brandy can also be dribbled over the tart, or drunk, or left for the angels.

5) Bake the tart in the pre-heated oven for 35 minutes, until the frangipane has set.

6) Warm the apricot jam with a drop of water and brush over the tart.

Rhubarb and Strawberry Compote

This is a perfect, light, summer dessert for June, when rhubarb is plentiful and English strawberries are at their delicious best. I like to eat this as it is, particularly after a rich main course, but it's also good with cream or Greek yogurt or, more elaborately, with Gingerbread (see page 160).

SERVES 6

450 g (1 lb) rhubarb, chopped
1 chunk stem ginger, finely chopped
75 g (3 oz) caster sugar
225 g (8 oz) strawberries, hulled and halved

1) Put the rhubarb, ginger and sugar into a pan and cook over a low heat until the rhubarb is pulpy. Allow to cool.

2) Mix the rhubarb with the strawberries. Serve either chilled or at room temperature.

Cakes and Cookies

Alice Waters' Chocolate Cake

Dark and Light Chocolate Truffle Cake

Gingerbread

Beacon Hill Chocolate Brownies

Sticky Date Cake

Strawberry and Lemon Cheesecake

Lesley's Sticky Lemon Cake

Banana and Pecan Muffins

Chocolate Chip Cookies

Alice Waters' Chocolate Cake

This is a very simple and moist chocolate cake from the founder of the famous Chez Panisse restaurant in California. Her style of cooking is based on simple but careful treatment of good ingredients, and it is important to use good chocolate for this cake.

Cooking chocolates normally give the percentage of cocoa solids they contain on their packaging, and most good, ordinary cooking chocolate is around the 50 per cent mark. A more seriously chocolatey confection may have around 70 per cent cocoa solids. Once you start getting above that level of cocoa solids, the chocolate is no longer (to my taste) good to eat on its own, as it becomes quite bitter, and using such chocolate in cooking may mean you need to increase the amount of sugar you use. In the USA there is something called 'Baker's chocolate', which tastes as if it is virtually 100 per cent cocoa (the packet does not give the percentage) and I find it quite disgusting when uncooked, but not only does it come ready divided into 25-g (1-oz) squares, but it makes the most superb chocolate brownies, so stock up if you are over there.

SERVES 8

225 g (8 oz) unsalted butter
175 g (6 oz) good-quality dark chocolate (see above)
8 eggs, separated
200 g (7 oz) caster sugar
50 g (2 oz) plain white flour
40 g (1½ oz) ground almonds
1 tsp cream of tartar
Icing sugar, for dusting
Crème fraîche, to serve

1) Grease and line a 23-cm (9-in) round spring-release cake tin. Pre-heat the oven to 190°C/375°F/Gas 5.

2) Melt the butter and chocolate together in a pan, then set aside.

3) Beat the egg yolks and sugar together until just mixed. Stir this mixture into the melted chocolate and butter, then stir in the flour and ground almonds.

4) Put the egg whites into a large metal bowl and warm slightly on the stove. Remove from the heat and add the cream of tartar. Beat until creamy with soft peaks.

5) Fold the egg white mixture carefully into the chocolate mixture, then pile it into the prepared tin. Bake in the pre-heated oven for 40 to 50 minutes, 'until the cake is completely set around the sides but still has a soft and creamy circle in centre . . . the centre should wiggle just slightly when you shake the pan gently'. If when you cut it, the cake is completely cooked all the way to the middle, it is overdone – the very middle should still be a little gooey.

6) Leave the cake to cool thoroughly in its tin. Transfer to a plate and dust with icing sugar. Serve each slice with a spoonful of crème fraîche.

Dark and Light Chocolate Truffle Cake

This is adapted from a recipe brought to us by a chef who had previously been working at the 192 restaurant in London's Notting Hill area. It looks wonderful and tastes superb – two sorts of chocolate cream supported by a sponge base soaked in coffee and brandy. If you have a little juice left from cooking plums or pears in red wine, it makes a lovely sauce to go with this cake.

If you are not familiar with melting chocolate and then adding flavourings such as coffee or brandy, take a little care over this process. If the melted chocolate seizes up when you add the flavouring, do not panic. This is particularly likely to happen with the white chocolate, which can be quite troublesome to cook with. If it does, just add a few drops of water or milk and keep stirring vigorously. Make sure that the chocolate has become smooth and shiny again before you begin to fold in the cream.

SERVES 12

FOR THE SPONGE

2 eggs
50 g (2 oz) caster sugar
50 g (2 oz) self-raising flour, sifted
2 tbsp coffee
2 tbsp brandy

FOR THE DARK CHOCOLATE LAYER

275 g (10 oz) dark cooking chocolate
85 ml (3 fl oz) coffee
350 ml (12 fl oz) double cream

FOR THE LIGHT CHOCOLATE LAYER

350 g (12 oz) white chocolate
50 ml (2 fl oz) brandy
350 ml (12 fl oz) double cream

1) Grease and line a 23-cm (9-in) round spring-release tin. Pre-heat the oven to 220°C/425°F/Gas 7.

2) First, make the sponge. Whisk the eggs and sugar together until the mixture will leave a trail when the whisk is lifted (that is, very white and fluffy, which will take about 10 minutes if you use an electric whisk).

3) Fold in the flour. Pour the batter into the prepared spring-release tin and bake in the pre-heated oven for 12 minutes, until golden. You don't need the oven for the rest of this recipe so it can be turned off.

4) Spoon the coffee and brandy over the sponge and allow them to soak in.

5) For the dark chocolate layer, melt the dark chocolate in a bain-marie (a heatproof bowl set over a pan of boiling water without its touching the surface of the water) or microwave, then stir in the coffee.

6) Whip the cream until it holds soft peaks. Stir 2 spoonfuls of the cream into the chocolate, then fold in the remainder of the cream. Pour this on top of the sponge. Put the tin into the fridge to cool while you prepare the light chocolate layer.

7) For the light chocolate layer, melt the white chocolate in a bain-marie or microwave. Stir in the brandy. The mixture will thicken and may curdle when you do this. If it does, stir in a few drops of cold water or milk and mix until it is smooth again.

8) Whip the cream until it holds soft peaks. Stir 2 spoonfuls of the cream into the chocolate, then fold in the remainder of the cream. Spread on top of the dark chocolate layer and chill until required.

9) For really neat slices, cut with a knife cleaned in hot water after each use.

Gingerbread

I once wrote in a magazine article that my wife only cooks ice-cream. This is a slander; Sarah also cooks delicious gingerbread. The recipe for this moist, fragrant and perfect cake comes (incredibly) from British Rail via the wonderful *Bread Book* by Linda Collister and Anthony Blake (Conran Octopus, 1993). It is delicious served with clotted cream or spread with butter or as a more substantial snack with a piece of Lancashire cheese and an apple. I am actually salivating with hunger now just thinking about how good this gingerbread is!

This cake is even better a day or two after it is made, if you can hang on that long!

MAKES ONE 900-G (2-LB) LOAF

225 g (8 oz) self-raising white flour
1 tsp bicarbonate of soda
1 tbsp ground ginger
1 tsp cinnamon
Grating of nutmeg
100 g (4 oz) unsalted butter, chilled and diced
100 g (4 oz) black treacle
100 g (4 oz) golden syrup
100 g (4 oz) light muscovado sugar
300 ml (½ pint) milk
1 egg, beaten

1) Grease and line a 900-g (2-lb) loaf tin. Pre-heat the oven to 180°C/350°F/Gas 4.

2) Put all the dry ingredients, except the sugar, and the butter into a bowl and rub it in or mix in a food processor until the mixture looks like fine breadcrumbs.

3) Melt the treacle and syrup together in a small pan and leave to cool to blood heat.

4) Dissolve sugar in the milk in another pan over a low heat. Leave to cool slightly.

5) Add the milk and sugar mixture to the dry ingredients and mix in.

6) Add the syrup and treacle and mix in.

7) Finally, add the egg, and mix to form a batter-like consistency.

8) Pour into the prepared loaf tin and bake in the pre-heated oven for 45 minutes to 1 hour, until a skewer inserted in the centre comes out clean. Leave to cool in the tin, then, if you can resist eating it immediately, wrap it in clingfilm.

Beacon Hill Chocolate Brownies

For some reason, now lost in the depths of Place Below history, our hand-written version of this recipe is entitled 'Beacon Hill Brownies'. It came to us from a brownie-obsessed American and was, he claimed, the pinnacle of years of research into chocolate brownie recipes. (His other claim to fame at The Place Below was briefly attempting to work as a waiter for us wearing a sparkling white apron and nothing else.)

These are delicious brownies and very simple to make. The key points to remember are to use decent chocolate and not to overcook them – they should be a little sticky. For posher presentation, try serving them with some home-made caramel ice-cream.

MAKES 16

225 g (8 oz) unsalted butter
350 g (12 oz) cooking chocolate (see note about different types, page 156)
4 size 1 eggs
350 g (12 oz) light muscovado sugar
1 tsp vanilla essence
225 g (8 oz) plain flour
200 g (7 oz) walnuts, roughly chopped

1) Grease and base line a 23 by 32-cm (9 by 13-in) baking dish. Pre-heat the oven to 190°C/375°F/Gas 5.

2) Melt the butter and chocolate together gently in a pan.

3) Whisk the eggs, sugar and vanilla together for 10 minutes.

4) Blend the chocolate mixture into the egg mixture.

5) Add the flour and nuts.

6) Pour the batter into the prepared baking dish and bake in the pre-heated oven for 25 to 30 minutes. The cake should still seem not quite cooked in the very middle when tested with a knife. If your oven is accurate and you use the same size dish as I have used, then 30 minutes is absolutely the longest it should need. Allow to cool, then cut into 16 rectangles.

Sticky Date Cake

This is a simple and deliciously moist fruit cake. I sometimes have three slices for breakfast.

This cake keeps well for several days and gradually gets stickier if kept in an airtight container.

MAKES ONE 900-G (2-LB) LOAF

275 g (10 oz) raisins
350 g (12 oz) dates, chopped
275 g (10 oz) unsalted butter
450 ml (¾ pint) water
1 x 400-g (14-oz) tin condensed milk
150 g (5 oz) plain flour
150 g (5 oz) plain wholemeal flour
1 tsp bicarbonate of soda
¼ tsp salt
2 tbsp chunky marmalade

1) Grease and line a 900-g (2-lb) loaf tin. Pre-heat the oven to 170°C/325°F/Gas 3.

2) Put the dried fruits, butter, water and condensed milk into a saucepan, bring to the boil, then turn down the heat and simmer for 3 to 4 minutes, stirring occasionally so it doesn't stick.

3) Tip the mixture into a bowl and allow to cool down for 10 to 15 minutes.

4) Mix the dry ingredients together, then stir into the fruit mixture. Stir in the marmalade.

5) Pour the mixture into the prepared loaf tin and bake in the pre-heated oven for about 1½ hours. Check half way through baking and, if it looks dark, cover with foil. The cake is cooked when a sharp knife inserted in the centre comes out clean. Leave to cool.

Strawberry and Lemon Cheesecake

I have seen in a couple of places recently something called a low-fat cheesecake. To me, this is a crazy idea. If you want to eat less fat, then eat less cheesecake. If you don't want to eat any fat at all, then just have the delicious, fresh, ripe strawberries. If you *are* going to eat cheesecake, though, especially if you are going to the trouble of cooking it yourself, then make it a proper one.

This is a proper cheesecake, and you will find that a little goes a long way. It is a straightforward recipe with a delicious tang of lemon in it, adapted from a recipe brought to us by a marvellous, manic, Scottish chef who worked with us for several years – Ashley Mackie.

All summer fruits go well with cheesecake, especially raspberries and strawberries. If you want to try something more exotic, make a purée of really ripe mango and fresh lime juice and use that either as a topping or a sauce.

SERVES 8

FOR THE BASE

75 g (3 oz) plain wholemeal flour
75 g (3 oz) oats
75 g (3 oz) unsalted butter, melted
40 g (1½ oz) demerara sugar

FOR THE TOPPING

450 g (1 lb) cream cheese
350 g (12 oz) sour cream
175 g (6 oz) caster sugar
3 eggs
Juice and zest of 3 lemons
350 g (12 oz) strawberries, hulled and halved
50 g (2 oz) redcurrant jelly

1) Grease and line a 23-cm (9-in) round spring-release cake tin. Pre-heat the oven to 180°C/350°F/Gas 4.

2) To make the base, mix all the base ingredients together and press into the base of the prepared tin. Bake in the pre-heated oven for 15 to 20 minutes, until golden brown. Leave the oven on.

3) To make the topping, mix all the topping ingredients, except the strawberries and redcurrant jelly, together until smooth. Pour on top of the cooked base. Cook in the pre-heated oven for 50 minutes to 1 hour, until the topping has set.

4) Leave to cool, then arrange the strawberries on top, cut side down, in concentric circles. Warm the redcurrant jelly – either in a small pan or in the microwave – until it has become a little bit runny and brush on to the strawberries and any little gaps between them. Chill thoroughly before serving. Cut through the strawberries quite carefully with a sawing motion so each slice looks good.

Lesley's Sticky Lemon Cake

Lesley Pearce has done everything at The Place Below – she has cooked, washed up, cleaned, waitressed, given massage and counselling. And that's all in her spare time!

I first ate this lemon cake at her house one summer teatime and, since then, we have made it at the restaurant many times. I like it *extremely* sticky, so if you like it more cakey, cut down on the amount of syrup drizzled on top.

For a bit of extra summer fruitiness, serve this cake with some fresh strawberries as well.

MAKES 16 PORTIONS

FOR THE CAKE

225 g (8 oz) unsalted butter
350 g (12 oz) caster sugar
4 eggs, lightly beaten
350 g (12 oz) plain white flour
4 tsp baking powder
Zest and juice of 2 lemons

FOR THE SYRUP

150 g (5 oz) icing sugar
Zest and juice of 2 lemons (or more, to give 150 ml/¼ pint juice)

1) Grease and baseline a 23 by 32-cm (9 by 13-in) baking dish. Pre-heat the oven to 180°C/350°F/Gas 4.

2) Cream the butter and sugar until fluffy.

3) Add the eggs and half the flour and mix well.

4) Add the rest of the flour, baking powder and zest and juice of the lemons.

5) Put the mixture into the prepared baking dish and bake in the pre-heated oven for 30 to 40 minutes, until a sharp knife inserted in the centre comes out clean.

6) Meanwhile, mix the syrup ingredients together. When the cake is cooked and while it is still warm, prick it all over with a fork, going right to the bottom of the cake, and pour the syrup evenly over it. Serve straight from the dish, cut into 16 pieces.

Banana and Pecan Muffins

These are a relatively recent addition to The Place Below's repertoire. We now make them every morning and people come in and pick one up on their way to work.

MAKES 12

350 g (12 oz) plain white flour
1 tsp ground ginger
1 tsp ground cinnamon
1 tbsp baking powder
150 g (5 oz) unsalted butter, softened
2 medium, ripe bananas
3 eggs
175 g (6 oz) light muscovado sugar
150 g (5 oz) pecan nuts, shelled and chopped
100 g (4 oz) raisins (preferably Lexia)
150–175 ml (5–6 fl oz) milk

1) Pre-heat the oven to 200°C/400°F/Gas 6.

2) Put the flour, ginger, cinnamon and baking powder into a bowl and mix together thoroughly.

3) Whizz the butter, bananas, eggs and sugar together in a food processor. Add this to the flour mixture, together with the pecan nuts and raisins. Mix with enough of the milk to achieve a soft dropping consistency (you will probably need nearly all of it, but it depends on the bananas).

4) Divide the mixture between 12 paper muffin cases set in muffin or fairy cake tins and bake in the pre-heated oven for 20 to 25 minutes, until risen and golden.

Chocolate Chip Cookies

When I was a child, for three memorable summers, we went to stay with my Grandfather, who lived in great luxury in upstate New York. Every day at 10.30 in the morning and 3.30 in the afternoon, a silver handbell would be rung to summon everyone in the house and garden (including children and a whole pack of neighbouring dogs) for tea. In the morning, we were given Sarah Lee pecan cake, which I thought was pretty good, but in the afternoon there was always a huge plateful (although actually never huge enough) of the most delicious home-made chocolate chip cookies.

After much testing, I think I have come up with a cookie that lives up to my own memories and we now bake them every morning at The Place Below.

MAKES ABOUT 20 COOKIES

100 g (4 oz) unsalted butter
225 g (8 oz) light muscovado sugar
1 egg
175 g (6 oz) plain white flour
½ tsp salt
½ tsp bicarbonate of soda
25 g (1 oz) walnuts or toasted hazelnuts, chopped
75 g (3 oz) good-quality chocolate chips

1) Pre-heat the oven to 200°C/400°F/Gas 6.

2) In a food processor, cream the butter and sugar together until lighter and fluffy.

3) Add the egg and whizz again.

4) In a separate bowl, mix the flour, salt and bicarbonate of soda together, then add this to the butter mixture and whizz again.

5) Spoon the mixture into the bowl, then stir in the nuts and chocolate chips.

6) Line a baking sheet with silicone paper or baking parchment. Use a teaspoon to put walnut-sized mounds of the mixture onto the baking sheet, leaving a good space between each one as the mixture will spread as it bakes.

7) Bake in the pre-heated oven for about 10 minutes, until golden. Allow to cool on a rack.

8) Find an air-tight container – and a secret hiding place – to store them in!

Index